Going Prepared

A Unique Church-Based Approach
To Crisis Prevention for
Short-Term Mission Teams

Forward by Dr. Crawford W. Loritts, Jr.

Lee Jacobs   **Steve Vereb**

Going Prepared
A Unique Church-Based Approach to Crisis Prevention
for Short-Term Mission Teams
by Lee Jacobs and Stephen Vereb

Printed in the United States of America

ISBN 9781609575205

Unless otherwise indicated, Bible quotations are taken from *The Amplified Bible.* Copyright © 1987 by The Zondervan Corporation and The Lockman Foundation.

Photography Credits:
Chris Jacobs, Chris Jacobs Photography, Marietta, GA
Bill Womack, Alpharetta, Georgia
Steve Vereb, Steve Vereb Photography, Marietta, GA

www.xulonpress.com

Dedication

————∞∞∞————

We dedicate this book to our families. Our prayer is that this will be an encouragement for our wives, our children, our grandchildren – and their children – to heed God's commandment to *Go and make disciples of all Nations*

Table of Contents

Bios

~~~

Lee D. Jacobs, M.D.

Lee Jacobs is the missions pastor Fellowship Bible Church in Roswell, GA, and an infectious disease and internal medicine physician. Since the mid-1980s Dr. Jacobs has led health care teams throughout the world in support of various field platforms including unreached peoples and disaster responses. He is married to Deb and has three children and two granddaughters.

Stephen L. Vereb, Jr.

Steve Vereb is an executive director of Vereb, Hitt and Associates, which provides assistance to churches and organizations in short term missions risk mitigation and church safety. He retired after 30 years of federal special agent law enforcement service. Since retiring, he has led many short-term mission trips and is the chairman of the Crisis Management Team at Fellowship Bible Church in Roswell, GA. He is married to Lenore and has three children and three grandchildren.

Contact: For additional information visit ***www.going-prepared.com***

Acknowledgements

⸺∞⸺

W e would be remiss if we did not give credit to our friends from New Tribes Mission, Guy and Ruth Seir and Bob Bowman. The Seirs and Bob responded to our call for assistance and subsequently became our catalysts and content experts in developing our program at Fellowship Bible Church.

We also want to thank our wives who have been encouraging throughout the process of making this book happen.

Forward

—◦◦◦—

Five years ago when I became the Senior Pastor of our church I fell in love with the people. There are so many things that I love about our church - the sweetness and sincerity of the people, their love for God and His word, their heart to love and serve one another. But one of the things that I love most and that runs deep in our church, I guess you could say it is part of our "DNA," is a heart commitment to missions. Besides partnering with various missionaries and agencies, year after year hundreds of our people go on short-term missions projects here in the United States as well as to many other parts of the world.

These short-term missions experiences have been life transforming. I love hearing the stories from our teams returning from their trips. God teaches us so much when we are willing to trust Him and make ourselves available to listen and learn and to be used of Him. As the saying goes, there's nothing like it!

There are also risks. Several years ago one of our teams ministering in Kenya was van-jacked at gunpoint. After several hours they were miraculously released without physical harm. But they had been traumatized. When they returned we cared for them and obviously our leaders asked a ton of questions. We wanted to know more of what had happened and why it happened.

And we certainly wanted to know what precautions we should take in the future to protect our teams.

Dr. Lee Jacobs (our Missions Pastor) and Steve Vereb (a leader in our church) gave leadership to an effort to help us with crisis prevention. During their research they discovered that there was a real need for someone to provide to the church a helpful resource for crisis prevention for church-based missions teams. So they decided to write it.

Lee and Steve have given a wonderful and I believe a life-saving gift to the church. They have given us a workable, well thought-through way of anticipating eventualities and how churches can or should respond. It is a wonderful tool to help us to be good, responsible stewards of the people God has entrusted to our care. Your church or organization will greatly benefit from their insights and suggestions.

One final word. The world is an increasingly dangerous place. No matter what we do or the precautions that we take some of us will be harmed or perhaps even martyred for the sake of the gospel. But this does not mean that God wants us to be reckless, foolish and unwise about our lives and how we approach the opportunities He places before us. The book of Nehemiah encourages us to build the wall but watch our backs. And Going Prepared is a great resource to help us to be obedient and wise.

Dr. Crawford W. Loritts, Jr.
Author, Speaker, Radio Host
Sr. Pastor Fellowship Bible Church
Roswell, GA

Preface

⚯

This book is a result of a journey that started in 2005 when a short-term mission team from our church was van-jacked in Kenya. It was quite an awakening for us. We very quickly learned that we were not prepared to deal with this major crisis. Despite having fairly significant experience in leadership, and extensive involvement in mission trips over the many years, it was obvious retrospectively that the appropriate steps that should have been taken were not at all intuitive. We made mistakes – several mistakes - big mistakes. It was only much later we realized that we inadvertently had created several preventable secondary crises because of how we chose to respond to the initial event.

During the months following the incident, those of us involved in missions at Fellowship were facing the reality that this could happen again to any of the teams going out from our church. Needless to say, the Kenya incident was a wake-up call. We could not avoid the sense that there must be well-established steps to take to both diminish the risk of a crisis developing during these short-term mission trips as well as to more appropriately deal with a crisis when it does happen.

Lee: I remember thinking – *there must be church-based crisis prevention programs available. Certainly churches must have already addressed this need. Considering the vast number of people going around the world on short-*

term mission teams from thousands of churches across the country, I expected to find an established solution for our church somewhere. I was unable to locate any such program for local churches sending out teams. It just did not exist.

In the fall of 2005, our journey finally took a major positive turn. Unable to find an established approach among churches, I contacted Bob Bowman, a long time friend and member of New Tribes Missions (NTM). We had heard of the extensive experience NTM had in hostage situations so we were hopeful that they might be able to help us formulate an approach. Bob in turn contacted Guy and Ruth Sier, a NTM couple with a history of intense involvement in major crises. The three were gracious enough to come to Fellowship to help us.

We learned much from our time with these NTM representatives. Not surprisingly, we learned how much we didn't know and that we had made several mistakes. We also learned that there are major policies and processes that can be put in place to diminish the risk exposure for teams while also lessening the impact if a crisis were to develop. Finally, we seemed to have some direction and this was encouraging news.

We also learned from our NTM consultants that churches and most sending agencies are not addressing this issue and are sending short-term mission teams out around the world at much more risk than the well-equipped, well- trained, full-time missionaries.

We followed up these sessions with NTM by designing and implementing a crisis prevention and response program tailored to meet the needs of our church, Fellowship Bible Church. We both feel obligated to pass along our learnings to churches across the country and around the world. Writing books has never been something either of us really had a strong desire to do. Maybe we just had not had a compelling enough story to share, but now we believe we do. We now have a message for local churches that needs to be passed along. That is the intention of this book.

Although we will describe the program in detail, it is important from the start that the reader understand what we are talking about when we mention 'crisis prevention program.' To summarize a complex process:

> *A crisis prevention and response program supports the deployment of short term teams by building upon a set of principles and processes that establishes a 'safety versus ministry' equation for each trip, and then for teams that do go to the mission field it provides steps to lessen the likelihood of a crisis as well as diminishing the consequences of any crisis or incident that does occur.*

This presentation of the program is the next phase of our journey – a journey not even close to the final destination. By listening to other churches that have encountered crises, and by learning from our own ongoing experiences in the field, we continue to refine our understanding as to how best to prepare our teams so that the Kenyan experience would not be repeated.

Realizing that there have not been experts in this new arena of church-based crisis programs, we believe that we are rapidly developing the expertise to be leaders and ambassadors on this tremendously important topic. Yes, much of what we recommend is opinions – but opinions based on decades of work in the field and research of churches that have experienced crises. So we present these recommendations, not to initiate a debate, but rather to encourage a dialogue that is simply not happening among sending churches.

Fellowship Bible Church's crisis prevention program is a testimony to the fact that the Lord does His best work through individuals who are broken – who have demonstrated as we did that despite experience and self-reliance – we failed miserably. He has taken our ineptness and He has helped us craft this message for His local church.

We believe that teams leaving Fellowship Bible Church are now going out much more aware and much better prepared for any unforeseen crisis that they might encounter. We believe that this program has helped prepare teams both spiritually and practically based on God's Word, common sense, and situational awareness. In summary, we believe that our short-term teams are better prepared to successfully accomplish their mission.

Our prayer is that other churches will be open to a dialogue and consider adopting such a crisis prevention program to better prepare their teams as they carry the Gospel of Hope to a needy world.

All the praise to Him!

Lee D. Jacobs, MD   Stephen L. Vereb, Jr.

June 27, 2010

Section I

The Compelling Case for a Crisis Management Program

—∞∞—

Chapter 1

Reasons a Program is Essential

⎯⎯∝◊∝⎯⎯

A question for church leaders: Why should your church consider developing a crisis management program for your short-term mission teams? Here are several reasons that we believe will answer this question.

The Magnitude of the Short-Term Missions Movement

First of all, the magnitude of the movement should get our attention. In *Christianity Today*[i], the proceedings of a very informative conversation between Robert Priest and Kurt Ver Beek are published. The opening comment by Robert Priest speaks volumes:

"Just how big is short-term missions (STM)? As a grass roots, decentralized movement, its scope is difficult to determine. And yet your own estimate of between 1 million and 4 million North American short-term missionaries every year may well be a conservative estimate. The sociologist Christian Smith, based on national random survey data, reports that 29% of all 13 to 17 year-olds in the

U.S. have 'gone on a religious missions team or religious service project,' with 10% having gone on such trips three or more times. That is, his data indicates that far more than 2 million 13 to 17 year-olds go on such trips every year."

The estimate of between 1 million and 4 million "may well be a conservative estimate" and "far more than two million 13 to 17 year olds" is incredible. Now that should get the attention of anyone involved in missions. Just from a statistical point-of-view, the likelihood of a team encountering a crisis is high.

How many churches are involved in this movement? Roger Peterson, in *Lausanne World Pulse – What's Happening in Short-Term Mission?*[ii], does an excellent job chronicling the exponential growth of short-term missions since 1965. Here are his facts on the senders:

"In the U.S. alone, there are currently at least forty thousand sending entities (thirty-five thousand churches, thirty-seven hundred agencies and more than one thousand schools) that do the sending."

In summary, thousands of U.S. churches and agencies are sending millions of people on short-term mission teams throughout the world. These impressive statistics underscore the significance of our belief on the state of team preparation by these sending churches:

Short-term mission teams are in most cases not prepared to prevent crises from happening nor are they prepared to deal with problems once they develop. As a matter of fact, we believe teams are drastically underprepared and as a result may be put into high-risk situations by their sending churches.

22

Although the statement may seem overly provoca-
tive, we believe it is accurate. Many are going; but most
are going unprepared.

Specific Reasons for Creating a Program

There are many considerations, but here are several reasons that we believe may convince you and your
church leadership to adopt similar crisis mitigation
approach to support your teams. Many of these points
will be expanded later in this book.

Short-Term Teams are Encountering Crises Around the World

As our church, and many churches around America
can testify, mission teams are encountering major
crises. The sad, and at times tragic, stories make this
case even in lieu of detailed statistics.

We probably could have intuitively arrived at this
conclusion by considering the risk one may encounter
by visiting any major U.S. city – especially at night. Any
leader taking a team to an inner city is well aware of the
risks of accidents, robberies, or assault and would be
expected to take steps to prevent these adverse events.
A billboard in our area noted the chance of an automobile accident is 1 in 8. Without knowing the basis
for their statistic, it is reasonable to say that just going
downtown in any major city poses the risk of accident or
hazard through the acts of others. We're surprised that
mission teams are going around the world into environments that may be many times more dangerous than a
U.S. inner city experience and yet their sending church
does not seem to be take precautions.

Taking precautions will continue to be important as
churches obediently send teams into high-risk areas.
In 1997, around the time of the kidnapping and kill-

ings of members of a South Korean mission team in Afghanistan, the NationalChristianPoll.com conducted a survey for *Christianity Today International*[iii]. The results are both surprising and affirming. Of the 884 active Christians surveyed, 69% supported U.S. churches sending missionaries (long or short-term) to countries in which military operations are under way (example: Iraq and Afghanistan). In response to the question: "Are missions to dangerous places irresponsible"? 63% responded, "Only if the missionaries are unprepared." We believe that this survey reflects what we have come to understand: that churches will appropriately continue to send teams to mission fields regardless of risks. Going prepared, however, is all too frequently the missing component of teams.

A question for church leaders and mission trip leaders: Are you adequately preparing your short-term teams as they go into harm's way? Crisis prevention is very complex, you cannot just "wing it" and send teams with excellence.

Secondary Crises Can be Avoided

As we have learned during our time of involvement in the arena of crisis prevention, very frequently the initial crisis (such as a vehicle accident or severe illness) could not have been foreseen and therefore could not have been prevented.

However, there are adverse events following an initial crisis, what called "secondary crises," that can almost always be prevented. Post-crisis confusion and exaggeration in communication can lead to a crisis for the team as well as back home that may be more problematic than the initial event. Secondary crises are avoidable with an appropriate program in place.

Spiritual Component of the Short-Term Experience is Enhanced

Although this was not an identified objective of our program when we started, we have been pleasantly surprised at how the Lord has used our program of situational awareness and safety tactics to underscore the biblical foundations of short-term mission trips.

We now have opportunities to highlight the mission trip experience as a *calling,* and are able to have a dialogue on other key topics such as obedience, trust, spiritual warfare and the necessity of prayer preparation. Certainly all of these biblical principles could be discussed during 'traditional' team preparation, but we have learned that there is real value in framing these topics alongside crisis preparation and response. Maybe it is simply that the audience is more motivated to listen and more attentive when these topics are presented in the framework of crisis prevention. Whatever the reason, as you will see in other areas of this book, this has turned out to be a very significant component of our program.

Reassures Team Members

Team leaders and members tell us repeatedly how much they appreciate the overall program and that they feel supported as they prepare for their trips. They are reassured that if they encounter an emergency, there are trained individuals back home capable of solving their problems. This reassurance is important especially when framed in a biblical perspective as mentioned previously

Reassurance may also apply to individuals deliberating whether or not to join a team. We understand that people join teams at various levels of spiritual maturity. Although trusting the Lord and going forth in obedience is the hallmark of a maturing believer, we are confident some individuals may join a short-term experience because of the added safety element of this program.

Reassures Families

Families, especially parents of youth, often voice their appreciation that there is such a program in place as their family member considers a mission team. We believe that youth teams are especially at risk if only because of the fact that these teams might be quite large with some teams approaching 100 members!

During a crisis, although the actual intensity of the risk is usually unknown back home, families worry that their loved ones are suffering in a difficult situation. It is very comforting for them to know that steps have already been taken to mitigate the problem when the crisis team from the church notifies them.

A solid crisis response program dramatically enhances communication among family members and avoids entangling families back home in a secondary crisis as mentioned above.

Utilizes the Gifts and Skills of the Congregation

By implementing a crisis management program, your church would be utilizing the God-given wisdom and the gifts of members who might not normally see their role in supporting missions. We have several additional members at our church who are now actively involved in making our short-term trips safer and more effective. We are good examples. Lee's training as an infectious disease physician and Steve's training as a special agent have been very complementary in this program. Add security consultants, insurance counselors, and others with related professions and we see that many others can have important roles in support of the church's mission of *going to all nations.*

Insulates the Church During a Crisis

In the midst of managing a crisis, the work of the church must continue and for that reason it is important that the leadership is insulated from the deliberations and decisions involved in resolving a crisis. Utilizing trained individuals (the crisis management team) to work towards the resolution of a crisis 24/7, would enable the church leaders to focus on church business.

This is so important that it is one of six foundational principles as described in the next chapter.

The Short-Term Team's Ministry is More Effective

We believe that the attention to detail and intense preparation necessitated by a crisis prevention program will result in more effective ministry.

In addition to protecting the short-term missionaries, the planning and coordination in a crisis program also provides the means for a more meaningful trip.

Decreases the Potential Detrimental Effects of a Crisis

Only churches and organizations that have endured a serious crisis understand just how widespread the fallout can be. This was a major learning experience we had from our time with the Siers and Bob Bowman mentioned in the preface.

We learned that in addition to potential adverse financial ramifications, the corporate emotional consequences could be long lasting for a church. There might be resultant media scrutiny and attack. A church that is involved in a crisis might also suffer fractionalization in the congregation, and sadly, a culture of risk aversion might develop resulting in disobedience to God's commandment to go to all of the Acts 1:8 fields.

Additionally, although litigation following a team encountering a crisis may be extremely unlikely, having a program in place demonstrates that well thought out steps were taken to prevent such exposures. This planning not only results in peace of mind for church leaders, but as experienced by some churches, insurance premiums may even be decreased because of the foresight in adopting a crisis prevention and response program.

There are No Other Programs Available!

Other than the approach detailed in this book – we are not aware of other options. Many churches are not considering crisis prevention except in a somewhat superficial fashion in that the distribution of waivers and disclaimers seem to make up the sole crisis prevention approach for some churches.

Since churches are not probing the safety question in-depth, and therefore are not engaging individuals with expertise in this area, decisions on whether to send a team when questions arise become discretionary. A case in point is the response of several churches deciding whether or not to send short-term teams to Honduras during major political unrest in the summer of 2009. Some teams still went [iv], some stayed home[v], and some came home early[vi]. Granted they all may have different ministry imperatives, but the fact is that a review of these situations clearly demonstrates the wide discretion churches use in deciding to 'go or not go.' Are all church leaders really in a position to understand these types of risks? This program can be very valuable as churches consider their options.

Conclusion

When we have presented this program at semi-nars and workshops, we have heard responses on two opposite sides of the spectrum with varying degrees in between. Most recognize on some level that the world has changed and that we as Christians must take some precautionary measures to make our short-term mission trips safe. However, carried to the extreme, these people would stay home out of fear, or would go but would be so restrained in their ministry approach that they would be ineffective. We are very concerned about such people on short-term trips.

Those at the other end of the spectrum have berated us for our lack of faith because they feel that our God is sovereign in all things and will protect us no matter what we do or fail to do. "Nothing has happened to us yet" has been a common response when we have broached this topic with some churches. We are con-cerned about these people also, and although well intentioned, they are often the ones we read about in newspaper articles.

We believe that as you read this book you will under-stand that the best position for effective ministry is to be somewhere in the middle – going, but going prepared.

Chapter 2

Learning from Others
Real Life Stories

———— ∞∞∞ ————

Background

Many, if not most, destinations are probably more dangerous now than ever before. In addition to the inherent risks of motor vehicle accidents, teams of Americans are viewed in many countries as profitable targets for robbery and even hostage taking.

In this chapter we will highlight several real stories, some tragic, in which teams encountered a crisis or potential crisis. Our intent is to convince church leaders that there is a tremendous need for them to take steps to prevent their teams from experiencing a crisis.

While we will be highlighting the principle of *Ministry versus Safety* in chapter 3, we want to make a point now. Understanding the complexities of the risks in mission fields does not mean teams should not go. It just means that they go prepared! As several of these stories can testify, situational awareness and the application of good old common sense can go a long way to changing the *Ministry versus Safety* balance well in favor of *Ministry* so that teams can safely go.

We believe that the following series of headlines and vignettes highlighting real life situations in which teams or individuals were at risk, underscores the need for a crisis program. Some situations resulted in a crisis while some detail an incident that could have easily resulted in a major but preventable crisis. There is probably no better way to make our case then relating these stories.

Headlines from Around the U.S.

These headlines are difficult for us to read because each of us understands the terrible pain and agony for families, team members and the home church. However, these sample headlines graphically underscore the need for both crisis prevention and crisis resolution.

Teen Dies During Costa Rica Mission Trip

Kidnapped in Guatemala: Mission Trip Turns Harrowing

Dallas Mission Team Robbed in Kenya

Local Mission Team Member Dies in Chile

Student Killed in Van Accident on a Mission Trip to Mexico

Specific Examples

The following are a few examples of crises or potential crises to make our point. All of these situations demonstrate how mission teams from sending churches are at-risk for being involved in a major crisis.

Motor Vehicle Accident – Central America

The senior pastor of the sending church related to us the following story of a crisis that occurred a few years ago: While traveling on an unpaved mountain road in Central America, three members of a mission team were killed when their military style truck rolled over. While this would be devastating enough, it is not the complete story. The first problem was getting help. Thankfully, after some maneuvering, a cell phone had enough signal to reach the U.S. Embassy in the capital, 135 miles and seven driving hours away. A U.S. helicopter initially could not find the team, and after refueling, returned to find the scene of the accident about eight hours after it occurred.

The loss of three lives was overwhelming but that was not the end of this tragic story. The U.S. citizen member of the team who was driving the truck was imprisoned for 30 days until the accident could be investigated. Someone else from the team had to remain in the country to make sure their team member was properly cared for.

Finally, because of a lack of comprehensive insurance, the senior pastor told us he spent the next several days working on getting the bodies flown back home. Regrettably, he said, these activities kept him from caring for the members of his congregation at home who were desperately in need of their pastor.

Safety in Southeast Asia

We both went to Southeast Asia with a medical missions team three weeks after the tsunami of December 26, 2004. The country was in shock. The foreign aid workers freely traveled the countryside in a province that had previously been closed to all outsiders. Muslim Shari'ah law was and is the law of the land. Guerillas and government troops called a truce in their civil war while foreign workers helped the survivors and buried the dead estimated at 225,000. We worked with a team outside the city where aid workers had not yet visited and in some cases where foreigners had never been. We treated malaria and physical injuries resulting from the tsunami. We also listened as survivors told their story over and over through interpreters. The emotional injuries would take the longest to heal.

We all realized that the chaos of the major disaster, the Islamic influence and the civil war made this a very high-risk trip. While we did take precautions, we learned that not all situations could be avoided. Steve's experience one night during this trip is a reminder of this.

Steve: The first night there at about 4:00 am I left my tent to use the bathroom. I used a tiny red light so I would not wake up team members in the house nearby. You can imagine my shock when I was lit up with a spotlight. We had not realized there were soldiers on the hill above until the spotlight stopped me in my tracks. The following morning we walked up the hill and "introduced" ourselves to the soldiers - young troops, some with flip flop sandals and automatic weapons. We think they were government soldiers, but we really don't know. We wanted to make certain that these soldiers knew that we were on a humanitarian mission and that we were not part of a military unit.

Traveling Alone at Night in a Dangerous Area

Steve: During our continued involvement in the 2005 tsunami relief efforts in Southeast Asia, the house leader where we were staying called a meeting to inform us that an international organization aid worker had been shot at 11:30 pm the night before, about 15 miles from where we were sitting. The female aid worker was shot in the throat while driving alone on a mountain road in a marked aid truck in an area of known guerilla activity. Thankfully, she was airlifted to Singapore and survived the attack. Guerillas blamed government troops and government troops blamed guerillas. The blame game did not make her wound any less severe. We'll have more to say about night travel later in the book.

We have presented both actual crises as well as high risk situations that could have developed into a crisis. Hopefully, for everyone sending or leading mission trips these real-life situations underscore the need to develop a crisis presentation program for their church.

It is our hope that in a very few years we would be able to state with confidence that *teams are well prepared by their sending churches and are not being put in high-risk situations for which they are not prepared.*

Section II

The Crisis Management Program

Chapter 3

The Premise

The premise behind our crisis prevention program is summarized in six foundational principles derived from our dialogue with Bob Bowman and the Siers of New Tribes Mission:

1. **Missions is a Calling**
2. **It's not about Safety, it's about Ministry**
3. **Think Stewardship**
4. **There is no Prize for being a Risk-Taker**
5. **There May be a Price to Pay**
6. **Minimize the Impact of Crisis on the Church**

We would like to emphasize that the process of formulating a crisis prevention program a church goes through is as important as the final product. This is why we discourage churches from simply adopting our policy. The crisis program of each church should be customized to meet the needs of that specific church and for that reason each may have different approaches and distinct foundational principles. Whichever is chosen, these principles should be the prime drivers for the program's content.

Let's take a closer look at each of our six principles.

#1 – *Missions is a Calling*

And He said to them, "The harvest indeed is abundant [there is much ripe grain], but the farmhands are few. Pray therefore the Lord of the harvest to send out laborers into His harvest" (Luke 10:2).

The first underlying principle is that *Missions is a Calling*. This principle underscores the entire program. The fact that the Lord is *calling* – is *sending out* His laborers - obviously has several important implications including the issue of safety of the laborers. This consideration would be for full-time field workers as well as short-term mission teams. Short-term teams being called by the Lord to a harvest field to minister is in direct contrast to going on a vacation or business travel. In the former, that fact that He is calling drives the mission. In the latter, people go forward with their own agendas of personal interest and satisfaction – and they only go if it is safe. Being called to minister on a short-term team has entirely different implications.

When we brief teams prior to a mission trip, we remind them that they need to be called by the Lord to go. Mission teams are heading into spiritual warfare. Prayer support and spiritual preparation is of paramount importance.

Deliberations involving all aspects of crisis prevention programs involve this first principle. When developing the program's content, or when deciding it is safe to send a team, or when responding to a crisis, the overarching consideration is that *Missions is a Calling*.

#2 – *It's not about Safety, it's about Ministry*

While we want to be safety conscious we must keep our primary focus clear. *"It's not about safety, it's about ministry"* (New Tribes Missions – Guy Sier).

This foundational principle speaks to perspective. We cannot be a safety-driven church where everything would be so tightly regulated that ministry is narrowed and dwindles over time. We wish to remain under the auspices of the Holy Spirit and be obedient to respond to our calling. So first and foremost, it is about our desire to reach all nations with the Gospel!

When we design our policies for risk assessment and crisis prevention, the focus is on the balance of the ministry and the safety aspects. When all factors are considered, it might be decided that the value of a ministry of a short-term team to a dangerous area outweighs any safety concerns. Our going to Southeast Asia after the tsunami in 2004 provides a good illustration. The U.S. State Department and most everyone advised against going there - it was a disaster area. However, the opportunity to minister outweighed the safety concerns. We took appropriate precautions and had hundreds if not thousands of people praying for us. It was not about safety and it was all about the ministry. We discuss this extensively in chapter 7.

Our primary objective in short-term missions is ministry. When we cancel trips, and we do cancel trips, we are not only doing it for the safety of the members but also as a consideration for what is the best for the team's ministry, the ministry of our church, and the field partner we serve.

#3 – Think Stewardship

The third foundational principle of our crisis prevention program is to *Think Stewardship!* Usually we think of stewardship as good financial management, but we also must be good stewards of the people and resources God has provided for His kingdom work.

Being a good steward means we need to plan our ministry responsibly, be well informed and have sound crisis prevention and crisis management policies. Our intent is to encourage a safety conscious culture while we answer our calling to *Go* so that we can be good stewards.

There are examples in the Bible where Jesus and the apostles withdrew to avoid trouble. In Matthew 12:13-15 Jesus healed a man's hand on the Sabbath and the Pharisees conspired against him, but Jesus withdrew. In John 10:31-39, the Jews started to stone Jesus for their accusations of blasphemy. When they tried to arrest Him, He "escaped from their hands." What about the Apostle Paul? He fled more than once, left by night, and was spirited away to get away from trouble.

#4 – *There is no Prize for Being a Risk-Taker*

"And from that time forth, half of my servants worked at the task, and the other half held the spears, shields, bows, and coats of mail; and the leaders stood behind all the house of Judah. Those who built the wall and those who bore burdens loaded themselves so that everyone worked with one hand and held a weapon with the other hand" (Nehemiah 4:16-17).

There is a difference in being prepared and boldly going forward as opposed to taking unnecessary risks. Nehemiah found that the walls of Jerusalem had been broken down, the gates destroyed by fire and the remnant there in exile and shame. In Chapter 4, Nehemiah reminded the Jews to remember the Lord first, and then fight for their fellow Jews and homes. From that point on, the Jews returned to work with one hand on their sword as they worked. While some worked, the others stood guard but the workers were still prepared to fight if needed. The book of Nehemiah underlies the premise of a crisis management program. We want to go because we are called (#1 Principle), as Nehemiah was called. It is not about safety but it is all about the ministry (#2 Principle). We need to be good stewards of those we are entrusted to lead (#3 Principle). Additionally, as so well illustrated in Nehemiah, we need to take appropriate preparations and precautions so that we do not take undue risks (#4 Principle).

Full time missionaries are not risk takers, but they do function with a mindset different from short-term teams. Their understanding of the sovereignty of God supports their calling even if it might put them and their families in harm's way. We all believe in a sovereign God, whether at home, on short-term trips, or in full-time missionary work – that He can use any situation in which we find ourselves for His glory. This truth is well communicated in Beth Moore's *Voices of the Faithful*[vii], a daily devotional comprised of the testimonies of how a sovereign God works through the lives of missionaries throughout the world. Again, full time missionaries are not risk takers. However, as discussed in chapter 6, unlike full time workers, short-termers have a different filter – their ministry might be changed, postponed or canceled.

Remember that *there is no prize for being a risk-taker*. Be prepared!

#5 – There May be a Price to Pay

It is certainly possible that for those involved in spiritual battles, there ultimately may be *A Price to Pay*. We believe that we need to be well prepared to prevent or minimize crises, but we also realize that there is a possibility that an adverse event – the cost - still might happen as teams go forward. The calling by the Lord of the harvest fills the gap between being prepared and this cost.

There are numerous biblical examples of paying the price, running the gamut from physical injury to martyrdom. Consider Stephen in Acts 7 and modern-day martyrs like Nate Saint, Jim Elliott, Ed McCully, Peter Fleming and Roger Youderian. They paid the ultimate earthly price for spreading the Gospel.

#6 – *Minimize the Impact of Crisis on the Church*

In the event of a crisis, it is essential that the *Impact of Crisis on the Church* is minimized. A crisis can have major adverse impacts to a church, so it is so important that a crisis is handled well and the ministry of the church is not disrupted. As mentioned in chapter 2, when the mission trip to Central America ended in tragedy with deaths and imprisonment, the pastor of the home church struggled to perform his pastoral and shepherding duties. He related that because he was spending so much time recovering the bodies from Central America, his church members suffered in one of the times of their greatest need. Just as the first appointed deacons brought food to the neglected widows (Acts 6:1-4) freeing the apostles for their main responsibilities, if a separate team of trained individuals from his church had handled these details for the pastor, he would have been free to minister to the members of his congregation in need. Such a team is an inherent part of a crisis program, and as you will read in Chapter 5, minimizing the impact of the crisis on the church is one of their major imperatives.

Chapter 4

Description of a Crisis Management Program

———∞∞∞———

Background

It is a challenge to provide a concise "elevator speech" describing the essence of an effective church-based crisis prevention and response program. It is not simply procedures or policies; it is far more than a slide show to train teams; and it is much more than the convening of a crisis management team. While these may be the most tangible steps – and each is essential – a sound program will have foundational principles and guide-lines to encourage a culture that considers safety issues but is primarily driven by the desire to have effective ministry. It is as much an attitude as it is a program.

Here is how we would describe the program:

A crisis prevention and response program supports the deployment of short term teams by building upon a set of principles and processes that estab-lishes a 'safety versus ministry' equation for each trip, and then for teams that do go to the mission field, it provides steps to lessen the likelihood of a crisis as well as diminishing the consequences of any incident that does occur.

Creating a Program for Your Church

A Program Champion

Any of you involved in church business already know that to successfully implement a new program, the first prerequisite is that a leader must step forward to champion the need. The person may be a volunteer or staff person, but as is true with any champion, he or she must have a passion for the idea and a vision for what a successful program will accomplish along with the support of church leaders. We have seen from personal experience that designing and implementing a new crisis program is both time-consuming, and at times, stressful. The program champion will need to persist in the face of frustrating barriers that will most certainly be encountered.

Design Steps for Program Development

As a church develops a crisis program to support their short-term teams, there are some specific design steps to consider:

1. The church leadership would necessarily have to understand and support the imperatives of the program. An essential and critical first step. Clarity of roles of leadership is of paramount importance and should be addressed in your guidelines.
2. It will be important to realize that some aspects of the program might challenge the culture of how the church normally functions. For example, making it mandatory that team members attend a pre-trip crisis briefing may be troubling to some.

3. Devise relevant guidelines and a policy as outlined in this book that meets the needs for your church's vision.
4. Identify and convene a Crisis Management Team (CMT), train them in the intricacies of crisis prevention and response, and then develop a process ensuring that a CMT member is available 24/7 for the short-term teams in the field.
5. Develop curriculum and implement training for team leaders and members.
6. Continually assess the effectiveness of your program and make adjustments as needed.

Our Policies and Guidelines – *Overview*

We want to emphasize again, that while this book does provide foundational information, your church should go through a process that results in a program tailored to meet its specific needs. The following is the executive summary from Fellowship Bible Church's Crisis Management Program that provides a good outline of our program. Each topic will be reviewed in detail in future sections of the book.

Fundamental Principles

Policy Overview – This elder-approved policy is consistent with the vision and values of Fellowship and compliance is mandatory for all individuals participating on an FBC-sponsored short-term mission trip. The format of this document consists of two components: 1) *Guidelines* that provide the details and background to the policies; 2) *Policies* that set the specific boundaries pertinent to crisis prevention and response.

Crisis Management Team (CMT) – A pre-determined team of five or more individuals that oversee the level of Fellowship's crisis response preparation and then provides for a centralized response to a crisis. The mandate, membership and function are listed in our policy. This team will be trained intensively and will be the component of first responders that will determine whether or not to declare a crisis and implement relevant policies.

Contingency Planning, Risk Assessment & Training – Requirements and processes are stated in our policy for creating current risk assessments for each of the specific locations that teams travel to or through, as well as detailing the responsive contingency plans and mandatory training imperatives for each team traveling.

Response During & Post-Crisis – The details of the appropriate crisis response is detailed in this section of the policy and includes the order of initial responders, the components of *team member care* that commences as soon as possible after the crisis, and finally – details of responding to kidnapping and hostage-taking. We expand on this area in chapter 12.

Crisis Management Team – Structure, Role and Training

The Need for a Plan

Experience teaches that in the event of a crisis or emergency, the existence of a predetermined and structured response speeds resolution and recovery.

Governments understand this and make elaborate contingency plans for a myriad of crises to minimize the impact on their country. Missionary sending agencies know this and develop extensive crisis prevention and management programs for their workers in the field. The same should be true for churches sending out short-term mission teams. In the face of a team encountering a significant crisis, it is imperative that the church has a plan to handle the crisis.

In the absence of such a plan, or the failure to follow a plan, the organization is not only hindered in its ability to resolve the crisis, but new and secondary crises may result that can ultimately be more disruptive than the original event. Consider the Hurricane Katrina disaster and what appeared to outsiders to be failure of the city of New Orleans to have a solid disaster plan. For instance, how many school buses were lost in the flooding when those buses could have been used to evacuate people to safer ground? How many people were stranded in the flooding? Was there a contingency plan in place to use the school buses to evacuate the people, especially those in the affected area who had no other means of evacuation? If appropriate plans had been made, or if established plans had been followed, what impact would it have made on the loss of life and property? Crisis prevention and management is all about planning.

Clarity of Roles

As was seen in Katrina disaster, as well as during the anthrax crisis[viii] that preceded Katrina, there was definitely a failure to designate who was in charge during these disaster responses. Such clarity of roles should be the hallmark of a disaster response program and are critical to its success.

In the same way, inherent in all crisis programs to support short-term teams, there is a need to make certain the roles are clear. This is especially true for short-term teams because in the event of a crisis, many people are involved and all would have specific roles. This would include the team leader, team members, families, mission leaders, church leaders, on-site partners, and possibly several others. Being intentional on clarifying roles and responsibilities before a crisis occurs is essential to having an effective program.

CMT Structure & Responsibilities

The CMT is not a new concept or unique to us. We adopted this concept from mission sending agencies that are more accustomed to dealing with crises.

The structure of the CMT should vary to best meet the needs of the church and will be impacted by the organization of the staff as well as by the specific leadership model. We have patterned our structure based on general structures of mission sending agencies. Your program may have different roles depending on your church organization, but the five CMT members delineated in our policy include:

1. ***Chairperson*** – In our program, the chairperson is appointed by the mission pastor and is responsible for recruiting the other members of the team. The chairperson directs the activities of the CMT including their training and organization and is ultimately will be responsible for any decisions and recommendations made by the CMT.
2. ***Elder liaison*** – The assistant chair
3. ***Liaison to our mission leadership team***
4. ***Information control member*** – This person controls the flow of information related to the crisis. All media or other inquiries relating to the situation are referred to this individual. The CMT establishes Fellowship's response including the specific details that will be released to the church's leadership, public, news media, and relatives. This information control person provides the information to a designated church communications person since generally no member of CMT should directly face the press.
5. ***Research & resource support*** – This person has the capability of obtaining in a timely manner the

relevant information and necessary logistics to support the deliberations and actions of the CMT.

Contributing 'non-members':

Outside Experts – While they are not considered members of the CMT, and for that reason have no role in decision-making, various outside experts may be added to the team on an as-needed basis. This might include but is not limited to experts in hijacking, hostage taking, the law, and insurance considerations.

Other support – Individuals who would assume associated responsibilities such as logistics, media, family care, finances, and record keeping.

Criteria to Be a CMT Member

Overall, the potential profile of CMT members may be:
- Spiritually mature as determined by the church leaders.
- Comfortable dealing with ambiguity. Frequently adverse situations require decisions with only limited information.
- Not in the midst of any personal problems or for any other reason are not prepared to give the time and attention required.
- Able to make decisions in the midst of chaos.
- For obvious reasons, any CMT member with a family member or close friend involved in a crisis would be excused from CMT responsibilities during that time.

Role of the Crisis Management Team

Crisis Management Policy Updates & Simulations

The CMT convenes for program assessments and might include training such as crisis simulation. The team also provides input into policies related to short-term team preparation. For example, recently our CMT provided substantial information which helped in selecting a new short term insurance carrier.

Responding to a Crisis

As mentioned in Chapter 3, one of the primary objectives of the CMT is to isolate the church during a crisis. The CMT would handle the situation in such a way that insulates and protects the rest of the church so it can continue to function, while containing the crisis to prevent a secondary crisis. When a team encounters a problem in the field, we do not ask the team leader to make the distinction between a crisis and an incident. As a matter of fact, we encourage team leaders to notify the CMT designate on-call for all situations so that a dialogue can take place and a determination can be made. This step may provide valuable insight to a team leader who might be burdened and emotionally overwhelmed by the crisis. If it is determined that the situation is a crisis, then the CMT is convened immediately. If the situation is determined to be an incident, the mission staff would be contacted to provide assistance to the team. Most importantly, there is ongoing communication between the team in the field, with the CMT and mission staff back home making certain from the onset that everyone is informed as to what has transpired. Also during a crisis, the CMT would:

- Make sure the team is in a safe environment.
- If the situation is believed to be a crisis, steps would be initiated to bring the team home.
- Handle all the initial communication to family members to prevent secondary crises.
- Work to resolve the crisis involving outside consultants as indicated.

- Oversee post-crisis interventions.
- During a crisis, the CMT will provide regular reports to senior church leaders. However, during an active crisis it is our policy that the CMT chairperson, not the church leadership, is ultimate decision maker as events of the crisis unfold.

Potential Barriers & Challenges to Program Development

As in any change that a church or ministry is considering, there may be challenges in gaining commitment and in designing and implementing a meaningful program. Here are a few challenges that a church may encounter:

Complacency: *There is no need for such a program since we haven't encountered any problems.*

Our response: It is our hope that churches decide to initiate a program before a crisis happens to one of their teams. During a crisis is not a good time to develop this program.

Leadership Buy-in: *Is there any reason to add yet another church program?*

Our response: This is the reason we wrote this book! Leaders may not see the value in such a major change as to how they prepare their teams, and so it is imperative that a case is made using an approach similar to what we outlined in the early chapters of this book.

Church Size: *We are too small a church to consider this CMT infrastructure.*

Our response: We encourage any church sending out short-term mission teams, regardless of size, to integrate a crisis program for their teams. Small congregations might consider partnering with other churches to create a program for both fellowships or using outside services.

The Team Goes Out

Just prior to the team going out, a document is prepared for our crisis management team consisting of the following information provided by the team leader:

- Complete name of each team member
- Emergency contact information for each person
- Updated risk assessment
- Telephone number for the embassy
- In-country contact person telephone number
- Translator available stateside who speaks the language of the destination
- Airline and local trip itinerary
- U.S. Military base if there is one at the destination
- Time change information for the destination

This information is provided to the CMT and the church staff involved with missions and is used only in the event of an emergency. A church may decide to keep this information in a sealed envelope only to be opened when appropriate. We have chosen an electronic format since the information is immediately available to the CMT who have all been vetted by background investigations.

Items Provided to the Team Leader Prior to Departure

Satellite Phone
Each team is provided with a satellite phone irrespective of the availability of cell phones in the field. This underscores the value we put on communication with the field, especially if the team becomes involved

a crisis. Since we ask that the team leader to check in daily with reports as well as praise and prayer needs, the satellite phone is a lifeline when other modalities are unavailable. We have purchased several refurbished satellite phones and over the years we have already found them to be exceedingly valuable.

Medical Kit

The team is provided with a medical kit, the content of which are described in detail in Appendix A.

CMT Contact Cards

The team leader is given a business card listing the CMT contact numbers available to them if they encounter a crisis situation. The picture below shows this card as well as the other items the team leader is provided for their trip.

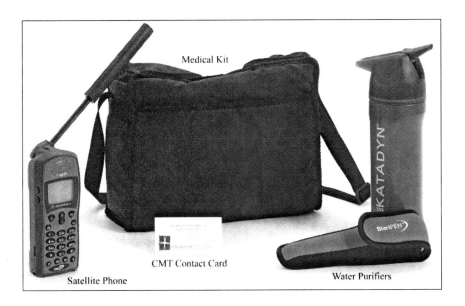

Chapter 5

Defining Crises & Incidents

———⊗⊗⊗———

Potentially disruptive circumstances for mission trips can be separated into two categories: incidents and crises. In the preceding chapters we illustrated some examples of situations that were definite crises as well as some high-risk incidents in which a crisis could develop.

Crises are those situations with severe or potentially severe repercussions – specifically, any situation that jeopardizes the ministry to which the team was called. Ministry would cease and the team would return home.

Incidents are minor inconveniences, or even serious situations that can usually be handled locally in the field or by the mission staff back home without disabling the functionality of the team. The team would continue to focus on completing their mission in these situations.

Here are some examples of varies types of crises and incidents, realizing that at any time the incident could become a crisis if the circumstances worsen.

Crises:
* Motor vehicle accident that potentially compromises life or limb
* Violent crimes, such as assault, armed robbery, kidnapping and hostage taking
* Natural disasters
* Major illness or injury potentially compromising life or limb
* Civil disorders and political unrest
* Imprisonment
* Terrorism attacks

Incidents:
* Minor car accident
* Robbery
* Lost luggage
* Lost ticket
* Lost passport
* Minor injury or illnesses

What all these crises have in common is the solution. For a short-term team the solution is the same – the ministry stops and they are evacuated home. Incidents are minor compared to the crisis. Losing your luggage is unfortunate but not a trip stopper. Passports may be lost, but bringing copies and having the telephone number of the U.S. Embassy can rectify this situation. This information is covered in depth in the planning and training phase of your preparation in chapter 9.

A Secondary Crisis

Typically a secondary crisis results from communicating at an inappropriate time or communicating inaccurate information back home to family members or friends during or immediately following a crisis event.

A secondary crisis may be created when team members or field personnel contact people back home before the sending church or crisis management team has a chance to receive the details of the crisis from the team leader. Family members need to hear complete information. For that reason, it is imperative that all involved parties in the field do not communicate back home until the team leader has given them permission.

There is also the concern that inaccurate information or partial facts might be relayed from the field. Remember the game of making up a story, then telling someone who tells the next person who tells the next person and so on. After a short while, details may be changed or embellished and by the end of the chain the story may be completely different.

This true story is a good illustration of a secondary crisis. A team traveled to a Central Asian country for medical mission work. On the second day in the field while providing humanitarian assistance, they were confronted by local police, detained, questioned, and finally released after 12 hours. During the detainment the team never felt that they were in danger and what actually happened was more harassment than physical harm. As is usually the case, the secondary crisis that ensued actually outweighed the severity of the initial problem. A secondary crisis was precipitated when team members informed people back home that they should start praying for this team because of what was happening. Prayer is enormously important in all situations but the information provided to non-involved people may create a secondary crisis as it did in this situation. Family members may hear exaggerated reports and become fearful before church officials are able to give them accurate and up-to-date information.

The need to prevent secondary crises is one of the most important learnings we have had since our journey started. During our interviews and research, we have learned that secondary crises are very common even though preventive steps could have been taken prior to teams leaving for the field. Although all crises cannot be prevented, secondary crises should not happen.

Chapter 6

The Safety versus Ministry Equation

───❧───

Safety versus Ministry

During one of our crisis presentations to churches we were asked, "Is there any place in the world you would not send a team?" We replied that we would weigh the risks using the best information we could acquire, and then we would consider the perceived impact of the ministry on His kingdom. Deciding whether or not to go would depend on the extent of the ministry to be provided, balanced by the safety of the field where they would be going.

If we determine the team would be under significant risk, and the ministry does not seem to be directly impacting church planting in a major way, we might choose to postpone or cancel the trip. However, if the ministry positively impacts church planting in a substantial manner – especially if the timing is critical – then it is possible that well-equipped teams may still be sent to minister in what appears to be an unsafe field. Here the potential impact of the ministry outweighs perceived risks. As a matter of fact, highly valued ministry almost always out-weighs safety concerns.

Occasionally we are asked regarding a specific mission destination "is it safe to go?" Wrong question! Obediently following the commandments of our Lord is not about safety – it's about His mission, it's about what the *Lord of the harvest* calls us as laborers to do. The right question is *does the ministry reason for going outweigh the findings of our risk assessments?* That is, *are there safety issues that might compromise what we are trying to accomplish? Can we still go and be wise and take precautions like Nehemiah?*

This balance of safety and ministry has been one of the major understandings that we have derived from our journey. Our deliberation on whether *'to go or not to go'* is always first and foremost driven by the 'right' question.

We believe that this equation is at the core of a church's crisis program and for that reason in this chapter we will explore the variables impacting safety and ministry considerations starting with the fundamental calling of mission teams.

Why Should Mission Teams Go?

So why go? What is the basis for the Christian mission endeavor? Why do we go out on short-term mission trips? The answer is clear when we realize that the God of the Old and New Testament is a missionary God. The Bible is about Him – His desire is that everyone, everywhere would come to glorify Him as His children. Starting  with His promise to Abraham (Genesis 12:1-3), the Bible reflects God's will that every people from all nations are saved (1Timothy 2:3,4) so that no one will perish (2 Peter 3:9). Finally, *"to go"* is a matter of obedience. We are commanded to go under the authority of Jesus (Matthew 28:18) and with the power of the Holy Spirit (Acts 1:8).

In the opening paragraph of his paper, "The Living God is a Missionary God," [ix] John Stott writes that the world is "hostile to the Christian missionary enterprise." Missionary work may be regarded as "politically disruptive and religiously narrow minded" and the "attempt to convert people to Christ is rejected as an unpardonable interference in their private lives."

Stott continues; "It is essential, therefore, for Christians to understand the grounds on which the Christian mission rests. Only then shall we be able to persevere in the missionary task with courage and humility, in spite of the world's misunderstanding and opposition."

Stott provides a good summation of this discussion for mission teams: "To go forward on a mission is His will for His people, and it becomes a matter of obeying God, whatever others may think or say." Anyone involved in domestic and global missions would agree with Stott, it is a matter of obedience.

Called to Go?

The mandate from God is clear – we are to go forth to make disciples of all nations. However, what about being *called by the Lord of the Harvest* to a specific labor, a specific ministry such as a mission trip?

As we discussed, a key premise of any crisis program is that missions is a calling. For this reason, a fundamental question inherent in this discussion on ministry and safety is whether or not a person is called by God to participate in the short-term mission experience. As surely as God sent Christ into the world, so does Christ send us into the world (John 17:18), and "as the Father has sent Me forth, so I am sending you" (John 20:21). The Father calls us to join Him. It is His missionary field and He directs us where to go, when to go, and what to do.

When we present our crisis prevention training, we emphasize the importance of being called to a mission trip. Leaders must stress that mission trips are not vacations, adventures, sightseeing for photo ops, or a way to fill your passport with exotic stamps and visas. Mission trips are the result of a spiritual calling.

Let's be clear – He calls us forward to His harvest fields for His purposes. It is not about us, it is not about our safety, rather it is that His will be done – His ministry - that the lost will know Him. This is why one of the most important guiding principles in designing a successful church-based crisis program is the acknowledgment that *it is not about safety, it's about ministry.*

Called to Ministry – Will He Protect Us?

As we present this approach to churches across the country, frequently there is a question asked or implied: Why prepare when God will protect us?

- What does scripture say about "safety?" First, scripture is very clear that the Lord will always be with us:
- We can be assured of His presence, (Matthew 28:19,20) The Great Commission, "Go then and make disciples of all the nations, baptizing them into the name of the Father and of the Son and of the Holy Spirit, teaching them to obey everything that I have commanded you. And behold, I am with you all the days to the close and consummation of the age." It is so reassuring to know that as He commanded us to go, He has promised that He will be with us always.

- Joshua was given a major assignment and was also assured of God's presence and that *"I will not fail you or forsaken you* (Joshua 1:5). God assured Joshua that any accomplishment of Moses had all been due to God's presence.
- We are reassured that nothing – not persecution, suffering or calamities - nothing can separate us from the love of Christ (Romans 8:35).

Secondly, we are called to serve in a hostile world:
- We are being sent to bring the Gospel of Hope to a world that hates us: *"I have given and delivered to them Your Word, and the world has hated them, because they are not of the world, just as I am not of the world"* (John 17:14).
- What could be clearer? *"Go your way; behold, I send you out like lambs into the midst of wolves"* (Luke 10:3).

In addition to the assurance that God will be with us as we go into a hostile world, the Bible is clear that we are also protected spiritually:
- And He sent the apostles into a hostile world but protected them from the evil one: *"I do not ask that You will take them out of the world, but that You will keep and protect them from the evil one"* (John 17:15).
- *"While I was with them, I kept and preserved them in Your name. Those You have given me I guarded and protected, and not one of them has perished or is lost except the son of perdition, that the Scripture might be fulfilled"* (John 17:12).

However, there is no guarantee that we will not be called to endure physical harm:
- In Acts, Paul's experience on his first mission trip to Philippi is described. A review of this chapter

will dispel any thoughts that our physical safety is assured. Paul was threatened (14:5), stoned (14:19), beaten (16:22,23) and jailed (16:24).

- How clear can it be that Paul and Silas were more intent on praising God (16:25) than focusing on their personal safety? Importantly, God used this persecution to reach the lost jailer along with his entire household. (14:32).

So God's purpose is that none perish but all have everlasting life. He sends us out and He protects us from the evil one, but His intent is not always to shelter us from all physical harm. God can use persecution and physical harm to fulfill His main purpose – so that people from all nations will be saved.

What is the message for short-term mission teams? For individuals, only go if you have an understanding that God is calling you. For churches, send out teams where the ministry advances His kingdom, always with the understanding the Lord will be with each individual and will protect them from Satan, and that He will use any trials and persecution to achieve His purpose.

It's Not About Doing – It's About Going

In the daily devotional, *Experiencing God Day-by-Day*[x] Henry and Richard Blackaby remind us that God has been working in our lives long before we started working with Him:

> *"Our Lord does not come to us to discover what we would like to accomplish for Him. He encounters us in order to reveal His activity and invite us to become involved in His work. An encounter with God requires us to adjust ourselves to the activity of God that has been revealed. God never communicates with us merely to give us a warm devo-*

tional thought for that day. He never speaks to us simply to increase our biblical knowledge. Our Lord has far more significant things to reveal to us than that! When God shows us what He is doing, He invites us to join Him in the work He is doing."

If there is one major challenge for mission mobilizers of people in the western churches, it is that so many individuals have the mindset that they are needed to go and do something – to fix what is broken. Although this is far from Biblical, this sense of *I must do something* unfortunately may be the dominating motivator for many people participating on short-term mission trips. This is not ministry; this is a task. Don't get us wrong – it is not the task that we are chal-lenging – it is the mindset on why we go. We are to fulfill the pur-pose that God has for us. We did not choose Him – He chose us! (John 15:16).

Stated another way, we don't make the Gospel spread throughout the world; rather, it is because of the inherent power of the Word of God (Colossians 1:6). The Indian pastors in the picture realize it is the power of the Word that has resulted in the growth of the church in India. The tremendous growth of the African church, or the church in China, or the church in Central Asia - has not occurred because of the works or the ministries of man. It is because of the compelling nature of the Gospel of Christ. God will get His work done even if we disobey His call to participate on a short-term mission trip.

What appears to be a conflict – *We are to go, but God can do the work without us* – is remarkably clarified by Paul in Philippians 4:13,14. Isn't it amazing that He makes the very familiar, powerful statement in Philippians 4:13 *"I have strength for all things in Christ Who empowers me"* and then in the very next, infrequently quoted verse Paul thanks the church at Philippi for sending Epaphrodites to him because *"But it was right and commendable and noble of you to contribute for my needs and to share in my difficulties with me"* (Philippians 4:14). Our powerful God can do all - with or without us - but yes, it is good for us to go to His harvest fields to serve alongside missionaries He has called.

Understanding the "Ministry" Component of the Equation

It is fairly straightforward for us to develop an understanding of the safety aspect of the field for which a short-term mission team is considering. However, we also must have a sound understanding of the ministry component if we are to have a robust dialogue in which we weigh the safety concerns and the potential impact of ministry. If we undervalue the impact of ministry, we may let any risk discourage us from going. That's disobedience. If we inappropriately overvalue ministry, we may be taking ill-advised risks to provide ministry that has little value or possibly could be postponed. That's unnecessary risk taking.

The first step in assessing the value of the short-term trip is having a clear view of the mission objectives. Most importantly the ministry must be "field driven" - that the ministry for the short-term team is ideally proposed, but most certainly supported, by the field workers. The local missionary needs to belief that the ministry will support his or her platform. Unless the church leadership, the team leader, the field host and each individual on a trip all have a good understanding as to why they are being sent, the discussion of balancing ministry and safety makes as little sense as it does to our non-believing friends. We suggest to team leaders that they collaborate with their field hosts and write a concise, one sentence statement on the objective of the team. This will help in any future safety-ministry deliberations.

So what makes up the "ministry" aspect of the decision-making process? A detailed dissertation on the subject is far beyond the scope of this book, and most certainly is far beyond our capability. However, we do want to present a few thoughts on assessing ministry impact since this issue is at the center of a church's crisis prevention program. Most importantly, the dialogue of safety versus ministry challenges how we think about our walk with the Lord and crystallizes our motivation for *going to all nations.*

Considering the Impact of the Ministry of Short-Term Teams

We understand that we must go forth in obedience, but let's ask a very specific question – how do we weigh the ministry component of the equation? Risks are easily understood and a process will be presented in the next chapter, but what about the ministry considerations?

We believe that the key point of the discussion involves the perceived impact of a ministry on the church planting movement. Although the extent of the impact may be somewhat subjective, it is important to ask the question *does the ministry to be provided by this team directly advance the church-planting efforts? If so, is the timing right? What would be the consequences if this team does not go?* These questions will help understand the ministry value side of the equation. Notice we didn't ask *how valuable in his or her walk with the Lord would this trip be for each team member?* While it is an excellent question, and one of the main reasons we are so supportive of short-term trip involvement, we do not use it as a way of assessing the value of a specific trip when weighing safety and ministry.

When assessing the potential contributions of the team to the work in the field, we realize that there are several types of ministries in which short-term teams may be involved. Common experiences include construction, medical and dental, national pastor training, orphan care, street evangelism and vacation Bible schools. All of these ministries have unique intrinsic safety risks and field impact that are considered when "go and no-go" deliberations take place.

A good illustration of the impact of type of ministry and risk was our Ecuador open-air evangelism trip that was canceled when the U.S. State Department issued new warnings for Americans to keep low visibility. While other types of ministries might have gone, the nature of open-air evangelism led to the decision to cancel the trip.

High Value – Low Risk Ministries

There are two other types of ministries for short-term teams that are exactly the opposite of the mindset that a team needs to go and to *do something* or to *fix something that's broken* as mentioned in the section above. These are:

1) Trips for relationship building and to encourage the local missionary; and

2) Teams that are called to a prayer walk ministry.

Although both are spiritually beneficial and very much appreciated by the field workers, in our experience the American church typically undervalues these ministries. Additionally when considering the safety component of the equation, these two ministries usually have a high safety profile. For these reasons, let's take a closer look at these two short-term mission trips.

What is the value of short-term trips going with the sole purpose of encouraging the full time missionaries in the field? The Greek word used for encouragement is the same word Jesus used to describe the Holy Spirit in John 14:16, *"paraclete"* – *to exhort; to cheer on.* Two points underscore the importance of such visits to a mission field for encouragement. First, the word *encouragement* is used frequently in the book of Acts as Paul, Barnabas and others traveled throughout the world "cheering on" brothers and sisters in the young churches. They all knew that the believers in new church plants needed encouragement *to stand firm in the faith* (Acts 14:22). Second, the value would be obvious by the blessings received in participating on such a team visiting a missionary with the sole reason to come along side to pray and listen. In light of our culture and the value we ascribe to tasks, the western church may not accept that such relationship trips are worthwhile. However, as many short-termers have experienced, the missionary in the field is very appreciative of trips that focus on encouragement. These relation-building ministries have tremendous value and again, tend to have a good safety profile.

The other potential low risk, high value mission trip ministry is the prayer walk. An exciting sign that the spiritual aspect of mission trips is in the forefront is that more churches are getting involved in sending prayer walk teams throughout the world. This ministry has provided an opportunity for believers of all ages, including mature prayer warriors, to actively serve in the mission field. When compared to other types of ministries, these teams require very little logistical support by the field hosts other than the usual basic lodging, food and transportation. Also, other than risks inherent in walking in a foreign town or village, generally prayer walking ministries are also considered low risk.

Safety versus Ministry – An Illustration

One evening in September 2009, after we had finished leading a pastors' conference in northwest India, we were invited to go north towards the Pakistan border to share with believers. The background that we had available when the two of us were deciding whether or not to go:

- As related to us by our Punjabi Indian pastors, Pakistanis and the Indians have been enemies since the Indo-Paki War of 1967 that resulted in the killing of many on both sides.
- At this particular time, our hosts warned us that Pakistanis in the border areas have in the recent past attacked Americans.
- The location is near the famous Wagha Border crossing where every day around 4:00 pm Pakistanis and Indians taunt each other across the border in an almost pep rally style.

This was the risk setting in which we both had to consider when we were invited to go north to the Pakistani-Indian border to encourage believers, many of them new in the faith, as well as to speak God's word to non-believers.

How about the ministry considerations which contributed to the decision "to go or not"? There were a significant number of believers living in the border towns and they were planning to hold the final night of a revival-type meeting that night – a meeting in which it was anticipated that many non-believers would be attending. As we had been told repeatedly during our visit to India, the encouragement of the believers by Americans is highly valued by the national workers and this would be an especially good opportunity to fortify the platform of the local workers.

We heard the risks and we understood the ministry. Do we go?

Our conclusion: When the safety and ministry were considered, we both felt we were called to go. We arrived at this conclusion separately. When we discussed our personal deliberations on the subject, we both felt that we would not have taken a large team there, and most certainly would not have taken a youth team. Although such teams might make significant ministry contributions, we both sensed that in the setting as we understood it, the chances that ministry might be disrupted because of a larger team was very likely. With just two of us involved, the risks seemed significantly reduced.

So we went. We wrote our report in the accompanying sidebar shortly after we returned from the border. You can see why we are so glad the Spirit led us to go and to minister despite some inherent risks.

On the Pakistan-Indian Border – *A night to remember!*

It had been a great day – but tiring. We both had lead the pastor conference for three hours in the morning followed by an afternoon medical clinic for church goers on the opposite side of Amritsar in Punjabi NW India. After dinner we were driven north to attend "a church service in which they would use a microphone (unusual for most gatherings) and many non-believers were expected to be there." We both felt that this was a great ministry opportunity that outweighed any safety concerns.

...and we drove north for an hour with the knowledge that Amritsar was already close, about 22 kilometers to Pakistan, so the direction we drove got our attention.

Finally we turned off the main road and continued on a dirt road – more of a path. There were no houses, just open fields. The next two turns were the same - very few houses. This is clearly the middle of nowhere and the night was already pitch black. I have to admit, and Steve later admitted to the same thought, *I think we're lost – and we're tired - so let's just call it a night and go 'home.'*

One last turn – onto an even smaller path and into what seemed like a dark barn. This is getting interesting...

Suddenly lights came on – and we saw the smiling faces of a large crowd of people! We were shocked. Apparently we were to be a part of a large revival for the area. They were saving electricity until we arrived. While we were having our local customary pre-service tea on the roof of the pastor's nearby house, we saw streams of people coming to the barn area, an outdoor area covered with large parachute-like material. The walls consisted of large blankets draped from support poles. For the twenty minutes we sat at tea, the stream continued. *Where are these people coming from?*

When we did work our way up on the platform, we had to walk carefully since this stage was made up of shaky boards covered with rugs and blankets. From the 'stage' – the faces of the people were something; the women on our left and men on the right – the children in the front radiating beautiful smiles. Difficult to know the number –with so many squeezed into each cubic foot – but probably at least 500. Then they started pulling the blanket walls down because the crowd was too large to be contained in the "building."

The first hour was a concert by a well known Punjabi Christian singer and young pastor who had been attending our conference. Our interpreter gave his testimony of coming to faith and the family persecution he endured.

Each of us then was given an opportunity to present the Gospel with special attention to the rows of men standing in the back of the giant tent. We thought they probably made up the curious but dubious element in the crowd.

> *While sitting on the make-shift stage, we thought about this amazing opportunity the Lord had given us to boldly proclaim the Gospel in a Sikh border town ½ mile from Pakistan.*
> Many came forward that night in response to the Spirit - some crying, some praying but all saved!
> Thank you, Lord, that you gave us the wisdom to go!
> Addendum:
> Two weeks later we heard on the news that there was a Taliban bomb blast in Lahore, Pakistan, close to the village where we had been...

This story illustrates the benefit of weighing the safety and ministry aspects in the determination to stay or to go. Others might have come to a different conclusion, but the essence of the deliberation would have been the same.

Safety versus Ministry – Differences of Full-time versus Short-term Missionaries

The belief that highly valued ministry always out-weighs safety concerns is the reason missionaries go to what many would think are not safe fields. And they would take their families! Why? Because of the compelling nature of a sovereign God's calling us to go to all nations.

You will see that throughout this book we contrast the short-term missionary with the full-time missionary since the risk and ministry considerations for each are different. Here is an example of a ministry versus safety deliberation that underscores the difference of the short-termer with the full time missionary:

Lee: I recently received an email from a friend planning to go to east Africa. She had just learned that she was about six weeks pregnant and would be twenty weeks pregnant when the trip was scheduled. She asked my opinion as to whether I thought she should go on the short-term trip. The full-time missionary in Africa had told her that he thought it was safe for the baby and the only decision was on deciding whether of not to take malaria prophylaxis as a pregnant woman. Here is my reply:

Dear _____,

No question - God is sovereign! I have missionary friends laboring with their families in what you and I would consider dangerous fields. They trust God and believe that any risks are far outweighed by the impact of the ministry to which God called them.

I believe God would ask the same from you and your husband – that you two would weigh the risk of the trip, the potential problems for your baby, with the potential ministry impact in which you would be participating. Full time missionaries are in the field committed for the long-term. They already are of the Spirit-led mindset that their ministry is far more important then the risks.

On the other hand, short-term missionaries are different. The timing of many short-term trips frequently are somewhat discretionary in that participation might be postponed or changed because the significance of the ministry might be outweighed by the risks to the short-term missionary.

That is why Deb and I responded as we did and were encouraging you to re-evaluate your participation on the mission trip. While you can take steps, you really can't mitigate the risks completely - the baby will be at risk. Just having to deliberate over the problem of the risks of malaria versus the risks of the medication to the baby tells you there are risks.

Again, because of their calling, full time mission-aries would tilt towards the importance of their min-istry; short-termers usually have some leeway in avoiding risks by canceling or postponing a trip.

Hope this helps as you and your husband as you pray about the best direction.

Lee

This situation demonstrates just how different the paradigm of the professional, full-time missionary is from a short-term missionary. Even with the realization that our God is sovereign over all, would a short-term trip to Africa be the wisest option for this second tri-mester mom-to-be? Framing the question as a balance of the safety with the ministry makes for a much more meaningful deliberation. Does this mean that pregnant women should not go on short-term mission trips? Not necessarily. If there are risks, and frequently there are even if minimal, then the risks should be consid-ered along with the value added to the ministry by the woman.

Disclaimer for the Nonbeliever

Generally the principles and approach detailed in this book would not only be relevant for churches but also to any team of individuals or secular organizations traveling outside the U.S. This chapter is the excep-tion. If you are not a follower of Jesus Christ, our com-ments here will most certainly seem illogical. However, we ask that you still read this section so that you will have a context for other discussion points later in the book, and most importantly that you will get a glimpse of the heart of the One who sends us out – our Father in heaven.

Chapter 7

Risk Assessments &
The *'Go - No Go'* Deliberation

---⟨∞⟩---

The Risk Assessment Defined

In planning a trip, it is important to determine if the team should go based on the current risk and the anticipated ministry, and if the team does go, how the trip can be accomplished as safely as possible.

Current risk is determined through a research process resulting in a "risk assessment," report that includes various items related to risk exposure at the destination. This includes such topics as the incidence of crime, road and vehicle safety, national climate and political situations, health considerations, food and sanitary conditions, ecological conditions and any other factor that may impact the safety of the short-term team. In addition to this valuable, detailed information on the potential risks where the team is planning to serve, these assessments also provide general recommendations to go or not to go.

Despite their value, risk assessments are the often a neglected portion of team preparation.

The review of risk for short-term mission trips can be broken into two categories: 1) The pre-trip planning;

2) The risks to consider once the team is in the field. Vereb, Hitt and Associates, a consulting firm[xi] in which I (Steve) am a partner, provides up to date information on the factors mentioned above while also providing a numerical rating for the country and if possible, for the specific location. This is the risk assessment.

Rating levels are different for adult and youth teams. Adult trips have a higher numerical risk threshold than youth trips for the obvious reason that adults can make personal decisions to enter into areas of potential concern based on the ministry versus safety guidelines. Again – the final determinations are based on the balance of the safety issues as depicted by these risk assessments with the overall perceived value of the ministry. In 2010 alone, several trips were postponed just prior to departure for reasons such as severe civil and political unrest, two volcanoes, a cyclone and mudslides. The missions pastor is the final go-no go decision maker based in part on the risk assessment.

In addition to obtaining a risk assessment when the team is doing initial planning, an updated risk assessment is reviewed just prior to the team departing. This step has been very valuable on several occasions. A few years ago one of our Ecuador trips was canceled because the risk assessment update accomplished just prior to the trip noted that the United States government had issued an alert that *due to some military action in the surrounding countries, U.S. citizens were warned to keep a low profile while in Ecuador.* The purpose of this trip was for a youth team to do street evangelism so the decision to cancel was obvious, but it was only because of the updated assessment prior to departure that we were made aware of the alert.

Another example of how helpful the risk assessment can be, was the information it provided during preparation for a team planning to go to Trinidad. This trip was to take place just prior to the country's presidential

elections during a time when the incumbent and chal-
lenging parties would be in very heated debates on the
streets. Included in the assessment was an important
comment stating the two shirt colors of the political parties, colors we most definitely wanted to avoid wearing
so as not to appear to be partisan. This was helpful
advice, especially since the color of the opposition was
orange, a popular and commonly worn color of some of
our Southeastern colleges.

Contingency Planning for the Short-Term Trip

What does contingency planning look like for a short-
term mission trip? Since the types of emergencies for
field missionaries are numerous and diverse in nature,
the contingency plans of mission sending agencies are
fairly extensive.

Most of the emergencies encountered by the full-time
missionary are not generally applicable to short-term
mission teams. If the mission trips are properly planned
and the risks adequately assessed, only a few contingency plans would be necessary and might include
cancellation for bad weather or evacuation for political
upheaval or natural disasters.

The Changing Assessments – Even When in the Field!

We were traveling by train from Delhi to Chandigarh,
India in September 2009. We knew prior to this trip that
there were longstanding travel alerts issued for India
due to the threat of terrorism, but we were unaware of
any significant updates prior to our departure. We were
given local newspapers on the train. The *Times of India*
front-page article for that day, September 19, 2009, discussed a Pakistani-based terrorist group that appeared
to be considering more action against vulnerable Indian
targets. Israel had just issued a new travel alert to go

along with the US, UK and Canadian expanded travel alerts on the same subject. Our pre-trip risk assessments had not been as alarming.

Here we were, in the field, heading for Chandigarh then on to Amritsar to lead a pastors' conference about 22km from the Pakistani border and in the middle of our trip we were learning of new risk threats. Our options were to turn around and return home or continue on with increased vigilance. Since our team consisted of four experienced adults and no youth, we decided to continue on. If this were a youth team, and if the alerts were verified, then the decision to return home would have been a likely consideration.

Nationals & Ex-Pat Missionaries - Input on Risk Assessments

Since most churches sending teams have field partnerships with national church leaders or ex-pat missionaries, we feel it is important to highlight some crisis-related aspects of this relationship.

What is the role of the national host in providing input to a team's risk assessment and the deliberation on "go-no go" considerations? Most certainly the frontline, in-country host does have a perspective on the risks that is not available to others. However, one caution in considering the input of field workers is that they tend not to see potential problems with the same eye that an independent examiner might. This is probably an offshoot of *familiarity breeds complacency,* in that the local host may be so accustomed to a lifestyle, such as ongoing violence, that they lose perspective. Here are two illustrations to make this point:

Illustration 1) At one of our workshops a lady related a story that makes this point. *She was watching television at home in the States and saw reports of continuing rocket attacks in the Middle East including an area in her hometown. What made matters worse, she recognized that the target area was close to where her family still lived. She called her mother and was casually told, "Don't worry, the rockets are falling at the other end of the street."*

Illustration 2) In 2008-2009 when the drug wars along the Mexican-US border had escalated, Vereb Hitt and Associates prepared a risk assessment for a mission agency that had missionaries in those border areas. All the major news agencies and governments were providing alerts as to the dangerous condition in border areas and our report indicated the potential for violent confrontations. We received a letter back from the mission agency extolling the worthlessness of the report since none of their six families in the country had ever witnessed a murder or gangland drug slayings.

So while we do value the input of the front line field workers, we also realize that their perspective can be quite different. For that reason, when it comes to risk discussions, we do not rely solely on the national or ex-pat missionary to make the final decision for us, unless they say it is too dangerous to come.

Whose Crisis Response Plan is to be Initiated?

Most of the sending agencies of ex-pats have their own crisis response policy detailing how the missionary should respond in the event of a crisis. For this reason it is important to agree on how to coordinate the policies of the team and the field in the event of a crisis. This communication on the subject of crisis management with the field agency before the team arrives is imperative. Confusion of roles on the handling of a crisis or potential crisis may be compromised if this pre-trip dialogue does not occur. Who takes the lead in responding, the host field leader or the short-term team leader? Is the agency of the hosts sensitive to the flow of information, or will they activate their prayer supporters (a set-up for secondary crises!) without clearance from the team leader? Again, these and other questions need to be answered <u>before</u> the team gets on the plane. Clarifying with the sending agencies of your host team should be part of your church or organization's policy.

It is important that the mission agencies of the hosting partners not compromise the team by activating any portion of their crisis response plan that would potentially include inappropriately notifying team members' families back home. If such pre-trip planning had not taken place, it will be important that the team leader and the field host coordinate their interface with their respective crisis management teams. We are aware of a situation in which the short-term team was actually trained and well prepared to restrict communication during a crisis. However, the sending agency of the host field worker initiated a request for prayer support in the midst of a crisis resulting in a significant secondary crisis.

In secure fields, the intent is to control the flow of information stateside not only to prevent a secondary crisis but also to protect the platform of the field workers and so that their mission would not be compromised. It would be tremendously disruptive to the fieldwork if the press was to report that "an individual from a church was injured while ministering to those in need on a mission trip to "_____" and the name of a secure field is mentioned. This would not be desired publicity for those in these fields and would most certainly compromise their effectiveness. Prior to a trip, this can all be pre-empted with an agreement that clarifies roles on how to respond to a crisis with respect to field agencies.

Section III

Preparing Short-Term Mission Teams for Crisis Prevention

Chapter 8

Selecting Team Members

—⊖⊗⊖—

Building the Team - First Step in Crisis Prevention

Team Leader

The most important step in crisis prevention is recruiting an experienced team leader from your church. Anyone who has mobilized mission teams understands that the success of the ministry is very dependent on the leadership of the team. It takes a trained and experienced leader; leading short-term mission teams cannot be a *learn as we go experience.*

We believe that in most cases a team leader should lead a team only to a location that he or she has been previously. Unless the proposed team leader has lead mission teams to the specific field, and through this and other experiences has demonstrated sound judgment and leadership skills, with few exceptions we would not approve a team going to the field. During discussions with churches, we frequently hear of teams and leaders all going together to a field for the first time. We believe that this is putting the team in a situation that may compromise safety. Additionally, it is reassuring to the team when the leader can take the group through a small, chaotic foreign airport and say, "Now we turn right and go through immigration." We feel so strongly about the team leader needing to have an understanding of the travel logistics, that we will have a planning trip of 2-3 experienced individuals going to the field with a team leader applicant so that he or she can learn the intricacies in leading a team to that locale.

If the location is a new destination for a mission trip, we use this same approach by sending a few individuals who have had experience as team leaders in other fields along with potential team leaders on a planning trip prior to the team going. Finally, as teams are organized, it is always a good idea for the current team leader to consider potential future team leaders as part of the team with the intent that they could lead a future team to that country. No doubt, an experienced and qualified team leader can be the most important component of crisis prevention and response for the short-term mission team.

The next aspect of team leader support is a training program that is relevant and value-added to the overall ministry of the team. We realize that asking volunteers to attend meetings is a challenge, however we have learned that face-to-face training sessions are still the best approach to coaching leaders – especially new team leaders.

We have an extensive training curriculum that includes several aspects of crisis prevention:

- Working with the host field worker to develop the team's mission
  - What will the ministry focus be?
  - Where will we be traveling? Our teams do not travel at night.
  - Drivers? National drivers, since our team members are not permitted to drive.

- Budgeting
  o Sponsorship letters for financial, but most importantly, for prayer support.
  o Planning finances. Budgets to be submitted three months prior to departure.
  o Deadlines. Financial requirements met 30 days prior to departure.
- Crisis prevention planning
  o Risk assessment received for the destination.
  o Plan transportation wisely. Cars or vans? Don't cut corners on vehicles – aim for ones that have lights, brakes, good tires and are overall in good repair.
  o Underscore the team leader's role in a potential crisis including how to contact the CMT on-call and how to lead the team during a crisis.

Team Member Selection

This process, after team leader selection, is clearly the next important step in preventing a crisis during the mission trip. The team member selection process actually starts with the training program for team leaders. During this time, leaders are coached on recruiting members for their team. It is a major responsibility of the team leader to put together a team that will successfully complete the ministry. It is a daunting task to build a short-term mission team with individuals who are called to go forward and who are spiritually, physically, and emotionally capable of participating.

Avoiding the 'Warm Body' Approach

As any experienced team leader knows, at times the shortcomings of an applicant might be ignored because of difficulty filling openings on a team. We all can attest to the fact that this *warm body approach* is dangerous and in doing so we can create additional problems. We have all learned (many of us the hard way) that with regard to filling a spot on the team with a person who for some reason is not a fit for the team, it is best to simply say 'no' rather than dealing with the consequences.

To help a team leader make a decision on whether or not to accept an applicant on their team, they might be coached to ask questions such as: *Do you really want to accept the person who you know has a disruptive approach to relationships and cannot function well on a team? How about the person who is somewhat independent-minded and might even wander off thereby single-handedly creating a problem for the team? Can this person handle the trip physically?*

There are several ways a team leader can determine if someone may or may not be suitable for a particular trip. During team meetings, the leader can observe how team members relate with each other that may give you insight as to how well they will be able to minister together. Also, there are various questions to consider when assessing an applicant to join a team. Does the team member have the temperament to make a particular trip? What if everything went bad in a location already known for its instability? Would an arrest for harassment in a far away county lead to a flare-up of a panic disorder? Granted, these are all worse case scenarios, but being intentional during team selection and observing each person's attitude during team meetings might help the team leader identify individuals who should be discouraged from joining the team.

Let's consider another crisis-related situation that might be adversely impacted by the attitude of a team member. A strong-willed team member can cause problems by initiating a verbal or physical confrontation with authorities. This is an important consideration because it may precipitate an incident and even a crisis.

Lee: Over the years I have had many interactions with authorities in cities and villages all over the world, and through these experiences, I have learned the importance of being respectful and patient. To illustrate, in the early nineties I had several trunks of medicines confiscated for three days by government authorities in Moscow. Since I was not going to provide a financial bribe, I was unable to make any progress in getting my trunks returned. After missing several connecting flights, on the third day I once again approached an officer requesting that my trunks of humanitarian medicines be returned to me. As he looked at my passport I was thinking this is just another stall tactic, until he looked up smiling and said with a thick Russian accent, "Atlanta, Georgia. Dominique Wilkins?" This from a man who spoke no English but loved his NBA basketball. I smiled and nodded to the affirmative, and mimed a jump shot. He promptly ordered his subordinates to go find my trunks and return them to me. I relate this story because I believe to this day that if I had challenged these Russian officials and did not respect their authority, I would have never seen my medicine again. I have had similar experiences with authorities in other countries, and I do not recall any situation in which being confrontational resolved problems. On the other hand, I have seen situations deteriorate because a team member challenged an official. This is an important consideration for team leaders as teams are organized.

If after much prayer and listening, you believe that an individual will not fit well on your team, you need to take steps. If it is apparent that someone is disruptive during team meetings and probably will not submit to team leadership, they should be told that they will not be going on the trip. With that said, we do not recommend that screening becomes intense or invasive for individuals. It is more a matter of being sensitive to the team member interaction and asking God for discernment and wisdom throughout this important process.

If someone is genuinely not suited for a trip and is seeking the will of God, He will let him or her know that they should not go on a trip. However, there will be others whose actions will cause you to intervene and tell the person – *no, I don't believe that this is the trip for you,* and then provide them with the reasons you feel as you do. For their own personal growth they need to know your rationale.

If we were to pick one major problem in team composition in which preparation for crisis prevention is compromised, it is the failure of team leaders or mission leaders to remove a person from a team. It is amazing how so many team leaders have difficulty telling a person – *"no."* We have learned that at times the team leader may need another person to accompany him or her during these types of difficult conversations. The fact that the individual may have raised funds and has a plane ticket is no reason to ignore this issue and potentially compromise team unity and the overall success of the ministry. We would go even further to say that if you have a disruptive team member after you are in the field, you may also consider that member's early departure from the field adhering to whatever guidelines you have for travel such as not traveling alone.

Team Members from Other Churches

We want to stress one important point on team member selection: If the team is made up of individuals from other churches, we encourage you to be even more deliberate in your interviews and pre-trip team training sessions, especially if the applicant is from another state. Requiring reference letters from pastors is also a good idea. As experienced team leaders will painfully admit, it was frequently the person whom they did not know well, and usually from another church, that was the most challenging to team harmony. Such dynamics may potentially compromise the team's response to a crisis or potential crisis.

Team Size

The variation in the size of teams going on mission trips is actually quite striking. At some churches, youth teams might be over a hundred members. To us, such large teams greatly increase the challenges of preventing and responding to crises. When we speak at churches and conferences we discuss what the optimum team size should be. It seems like the majority of churches have settled on teams numbering around 10-15 people. We have learned over the years that teams of 7-8 seem the most manageable, especially if going to high-risk fields. Not only are the safety issues less and the challenge of travel logistics minimized, but also the team interaction and opportunities for spiritual growth are enhanced. For many of our teams that go to distant fields where difficult travel and living accommodations can be anticipated, we prefer small teams of 4-5 members since it is so much easier logistically for the in-country hosts.

Whatever the size of the teams you determine is necessary to accomplish the ministry, realize that your decision has safety ramifications. The larger the team, the more difficult the logistics will be for the team leader and for the field host to coordinate. Just keeping track of large numbers of people during a trip is a difficult task. Planning with the host and honoring their recommendations is always wise.

These comments on large teams might raise the question – "What about those large youth teams?" "Spring break only happens one time a year!" The church leaders may feel that they have no choice, but whatever is determined to be the team size, we remind them that the safety issues have been exponentially increased when the team member count gets to be much over fifteen. The missions leaders might consider staggering the dates of the trips or splitting large teams and sending them to different fields. To be very honest, we cringe when we hear of teams of eighty high school students going to Mexico. We're sure that such trips have been and can continue to be a wonderful experience. However, from a safety-ministry consideration, all too often we see teams going even if the equation tilts heavily towards safety concerns because of risks. In other words, the risks of the very large teams are downplayed and the teams are still sent by the church. Just recently, we were notified of a team of several hundred youth going to Mexico over spring break. While these trips have been completed without incident, given the current climate of crime in Mexico and the logistical challenges of a team of this size, it would have been difficult for us to encourage such a mission trip.

Youth Team Chaperones – How Many?

How many chaperones do you need for youth trips? Chaperone numbers will depend on the number on the team, the age of the youth, and the gender ratio. There are many crisis-related reasons why we believe the chaperone ratio should be well thought out. For example, if there is a personal incident such as an accident or an illness not necessitating evacuation of the entire team, an adult of the same gender needs to be available to escort the affected person home. Sending a chaperone to accompany the youth is essential, since *no one should be put in the position of traveling alone.* If there are fifteen youth and you only have three chaperones, one male and two females, and a young man needs to go home, you are left with the potential of having to bring the team back home because the remaining fourteen co-ed youth will only have two female chaperones. This potential situation alone should cause leaders to pause and reconsider the number and gender of chaperones. So what ratios make sense? Consider one chaperone for each four youth team members with a minimum of two male and two female chaperones for co-ed teams.

Potential Member Physical & Emotional Health Considerations

The first step in preventing a health-related crisis is again team member selection. If there is any concern that an individual will potentially have physical or emotional problems with a specific short-term experience, *just say no!*

Be mindful of the physical requirements for the location of your experience. For example, if the team is traveling to a Himalayan village, then individuals with pulmonary disorders such as severe asthma or those who are out of shape should consider alternative trips.

Lee: In my experience, the physical concerns are fairly easy to verbalize and an individual would usually opt out. However, individuals with emotional health problems would be less likely to withdraw from the team, and so it may be necessary to involve family members or doctors before the person is given a "clearance" to go. We encourage individuals who have a tendency to panic disorders or phobias, such as claustrophobia, to consider opting out of some experiences. As we have all learned, a problem with emotional health is all too common an occurrence during trips and may be tremendously disruptive. Having open dialogues with potential team members who have such emotional issues is the first step to avoiding these problems. If anxiety issues are frequent and severe, the applicant probably should be encouraged to serve in their Jerusalem and Judea to get some idea as to how troublesome this problem might be in a distant mission field. For example, these individuals may gain confidence by participating in local cross-cultural experiences such as homeless shelters. Actually, serving domestically in a cross-cultural experience can be good preparation for anyone considering global short-term mission trips, and so we encourage individuals such as nurses to consider serving first locally.

One final health comment: We tell people that if they or their personal physician feel that they have a potentially severe medical problem (example: diabetes or heart failure), then we encourage them only to go to fields in which they can be at a quality hospital within 24 hours. While this standard is somewhat arbitrary, it does provide some guidance for individuals praying about which team to join.

Background Checks

Pedophiles and other lawbreakers all too often target churches because of historically lax security procedures. Although churches are becoming more vigilant due to the recent attacks directed at church services, there are still organizations that do not take appropriate security precautions. Churches regularly obtain background checks on individuals working in their youth education centers, and for the same rationale we believe that short-term mission team members should be similarly screened. We only permit individuals with a completed background check to join a team that our church sponsors

Checklist for Building the Team
___Experienced Team Leader
___Team Member Selection
___Physical & Emotional Health Considerations
___Team Size
___Ratio of Chaperones
___Background Checks

Chapter 9

Team Preparation

Team Meetings

Several team meetings are helpful in preparing the team for ministry by developing an understanding of the ministry goals, the important aspects of the host's missionary platform, travel information, packing advice, and importantly, the potential risks of the trip. For out of town team members, conference calls and *Skype* are most certainly better than no pre-trip contact.

In sports, to win a game every member of the team must have a clear understanding of the rules of the game, know their interdependent roles, and have a plan to win. In similar fashion, each team member must have a clear understanding of the imperatives of the ministry, the role of the team leader, their role on the team and the logistical challenges of being part of a short-term mission team. These can be important agenda items for team meetings.

Remembering that the team is heading into spiritual battle underscores the importance of team prayer time as well as the importance of each team member identifying people who can pray for them. The prayerful preparation is always an important step in team building as the team together asks the Lord to prepare the way. Teams may find value from an in-depth study of Ephesians 6:10-18, Paul's admonition on how best to prepare for spiritual warfare.

This team-based preparation is essential to developing a foundation for crisis management. The stronger a team is bonded together, and the more prayer support they have enlisted, the more likely their ministry will be successful. It is informative to include at meetings a dialogue about the risk assessment of the destination, as well as the safety topics we have been discussing. By doing this the team will be taking major strides to averting potentially adverse situations.

Member Preparation Meeting – Mandatory?

We have learned that team meetings alone are not adequate. As indispensible as these team gatherings are, we believe that it is asking too much of the team leader to relay the intricacies of crisis management that the church's missions leadership has identified as essential for each team member to hear.

So what is the best way to relay a core of important information to 300-400 people going annually throughout the world on numerous short-term mission teams? You may develop a solution that works for your church, but our answer at Fellowship works. We require that anyone going on a Fellowship-sponsored mission trip must attend a 60-90 minute meeting with their team no later than 30 days before the team is to depart. For youth teams, we ask that both parents attend a session. All participants sign-off that they have attended and they agree to follow stipulations that we raise during the presentation. Failure to attend a mandatory session before the 30-day time frame unfortunately means the individual will not be able to join the team.

Using words such as "mandatory" and "required" when relating to those who have volunteered their time to join a mission team might seem like we are adding unnecessary structure. However, we believe that such requirements have greatly advanced our teams in both the spiritual preparation as well as the crisis management aspect for their specific trip. Although some team members had expressed reluctance in having to attend a meeting, following the sessions the majority express an appreciation for our efforts. Parents of youth team members are especially appreciative.

We hold these sessions at a time of the year before the majority of the teams depart. Since over 60% of our teams go in July, and with several as early as April, we start our semi-monthly mandatory team meetings in March. The time is flexible to adapt to the needs of the team; however, the majority of the meetings follow the Sunday service. We encourage the teams to sit together as a group.

The presentation is divided into three parts, with breaks in between each section for teams to discuss content and to pray. The presentation begins with the spiritual aspects of the experience, including the importance of being called, the necessity of prayer support and the attributes of a short-term missionary. During the attributes discussion we stress the need to be flexible since the Lord might use the person in a far different way then they plan, the importance of serving the ex-pat missionary or the national host partner, and other similar reminders. This first section ends with the team sharing their personal prayer needs and praying as a team for the success of the mission.

The middle section of the presentation is the crisis briefing. During this part we discuss situational awareness and other crisis-related topics as outlined in this book. The most important discussion deals with one specific aspect of the crisis response policy – the role of the team leader in the event of a crisis. The emphasis here is the requirement that no team member is to communicate back home during a crisis until the team leader gives his or her permission. An agreement form acknowledging this policy is signed at the end of the presentation.

The final section deals with the teams completing paperwork, including all the contact information required by the CMT.

Enhancing Safety – From Fanny Packs to Back Packs to Shirts!

Team preparation includes suggestions for members on how to lessen the risk of losing passports, money and other personal items. Although losing these items generally does not result in a crisis, these incidents are extremely frustrating for team members and are generally preventable. Thieves are worldwide and will take any opportunity to relieve a traveler of their valuables. In some countries, pocket picking and the slashing of purses, backpacks and fanny packs is considered an art form and as such, there are some very skilled people stealing personal items.

Steps can be taken to decrease the likelihood of such losses occurring. During our team preparation meetings, we take the time to recommend that each team member consider security when they are planning which wallet, purse, backpack or daypack to bring on the trip. We mention that several companies provide travel clothing and gear that include slash-proof straps and tamper-proof locks and clips. Hiking stores have comfortable travel shirts and pants that have zippered pockets ideal for protecting passports and other valuables.

Here are two examples: The first photo shows a young lady who could likely lose her purse and belongings to a purse-snatcher, slasher or even a drive-by motorcycle thief. The second photo shows the strap across her body with her hand holding the purse from the bottom that offers much more protection than the first example. Similarly backpacks and fanny packs with slash-proof straps and tamper-proof locks should be worn to provide as much protection as possible from theft. Regardless of the purse or fanny pack used, we advise team members to keep personal belongings on their person at all times.

A few additional comments on attire: For safety, as well as to be culturally sensitive, team members should dress conservatively so as to not attract attention. We suggest minimal jewelry and encourage team members to leave rings and watches at home. Buying a $10 wedding band might lessen the heartbreak if a loss occurs, as does wearing an inexpensive plastic watch with a bright background light. Tattoos should be covered when in the field since in a number of cultures they are considered inappropriate for Christians or even for the general population.

Such advice on dress, tattoos and jewelry may contradict the belief by a team member who feels that *they need to accept me just as I am.* Wrong! You are an invited guest called to serve and encourage the national believers. If there is any question on what is appropriate in a culture and what is not, the team leader should clarify with the national or ex-pat missionary host as part of his or her pre-trip planning.

Plane Travel & Safety Considerations

Here are some practical suggestions on airplane bookings that might turn out to be critical during a response to an incident or crisis. If either does happen to a short-term team, these suggestions on booking flights will help support the CMT response.

- **All team members on the same ticket reservation:** It helps the team's interface with an airline if all members are on the same reservation booking. This will facilitate any changes in bookings when an expedited exit is needed or a flight is canceled. Team members leaving from different airports may be on different bookings. If this cannot be avoided, the team leader needs to be aware of the relevant details.
- **All flights on one reservation:** Additionally, having all the flight connections for team members on the same airline reservation is very important. If an airline cancels a flight, and the flights are on the reservation, the airlines will then assume the responsibility of changing all other connecting flights impacted by the change. If all connections are not on the canceling airline's reservation, they will not assume responsibility for changing other flights with other airlines. This is especially important if the team is planning on being in a location with only one flight per week. A few years ago our Friday British Air flight out of Central Asia was canceled and we were rebooked

on the next flight leaving the following Monday. British Air assumed the responsibility for moving all of our connecting flights on their reservation at no cost. However, we had booked our stateside travel separately on a U. S. domestic airlines and it was quite a hassle getting the changes made without having to pay major change fees.

- **Contact phone number:** Be careful in choosing which contact telephone numbers you leave with the airline. If your flights are changed or canceled at night or on a weekend, having the church's phone number on record may be useless. If it is your home number and no one is home to warn you, then your cancellation will be a surprise when you get to the airport. This happened to us recently when our flight into Haiti to bring post-earthquake relief was canceled. Since the contact number was a phone at the church, we did not learn of the middle of the night cancellation until we arrived at the airport at 5:00 am.

While having our Haiti flight canceled was not a major problem for us since we were in our home city, imagine the logistical problems if this happened in a developing country. If your flight is canceled in such a setting, make certain that the airline provides you with a safe hotel. If you or your hosts know of a hotel in a safe part of town, tell the airline that is where you want to go; safety considerations should rule. Most importantly and consistent with good crisis prevention principles, keep the team together and avoid night travel regardless of what the airlines might dictate.

Finally, all teams should avoid flying on in-country airlines in the developing world. When making your reservations, try to book them on an established, quality airline. Chances are the airplane will be better maintained and without duct taped seats as in the picture, and for these reasons will probably be safer.

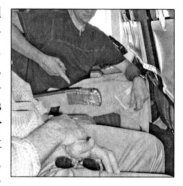

Team Members Driving in Foreign Countries

The simple answer is *don't*! Team members on Fellowship-sponsored trips do not drive while in fields outside the United States. While exceptions might be made for certain travel in Canada and Europe, generally our team members do not drive.

The reasons are fairly straightforward and include insurance considerations, safety concerns and local legal and culture considerations. For example, when an American is involved in an accident outside the United States, in many countries the American is considered at fault regardless of details of the situation mainly because of our perceived affluence. Can you imagine the risk you would be taking driving in a location with veiled motorcycle drivers as in the picture? In second chapter we mentioned the very unfortunate accident occurring during a mission trip that resulted in three people being killed when their truck rolled over. The crisis was bad enough, but to complicate a terrible situation the driver, an American member of the team, was jailed for 30 days.

This tragic story illustrated the problems that can arise from an American driver in a foreign country.

Finally, laws can be very different in other countries. Steve: I remember the trouble my father had in Mali a number of years ago. He had an accident with a local driver who went through a red light and was clearly at fault according to both logic and general principle. However, my father was cited by the authorities and forced to pay compensation because the other driver got to the intersection first. While such laws may not be logical, if it is the local law or custom, it is not an issue for debate.

We encourage all mission leaders to re-evaluate their policy if members from their church drive in foreign countries. It is a risk that can easily be mitigated and most certainly is worth the effort.

Decreasing Traveling Risks

According to the Center for Disease Control and Prevention (CDC), motor vehicle accidents are the most common cause of deaths and injuries to Americans traveling outside the United States.[xii] The contributing factors included poor roads, foreign driving habits, poorly equipped cars and vans, and of course – speed.

If you are convinced you that your team members should not drive, the option then would be for you to hire drivers and vehicles to accommodate your needs. With large teams, should you rent several cars or one van? From a risk perspective, in some countries it might be safer renting two or more cars rather than renting a large van. The team would be less obvious traveling in cars, thereby potentially being less of a hijacking target. This is especially true in countries where a van packed with people from another culture

would be a novel sight. No specific recommendation here, but we wanted to make sure you are considering the risk factors involved in this deliberation on the mode of transportation.

Anyone who has spent time overseas has probably been impressed at how creative the nationals are in jerry-rigging their vehicles to make it to the next stop. When making your arrangements, consider expanding your budget allocation and look for safe vehicles with seatbelts, decent tires and working lights. We have even invested in repairs before we took the team on the road. Overall, it is well worth your time to be deliberate in locating and hiring the right vehicles and safe drivers.

We strongly recommend that teams not travel after dark. In addition to the increased exposure to robbery and assault, there are a variety of other reasons for this requirement. These include hazards such as trucks with no lights, poor roads, people wearing dark clothing without lights, broken-down cars marked by nothing more than a pile of brush, animals wandering in the road, and a number of other similar dangers. We have seen large trucks driving down remote mountain roads at night with only a flashlight for illumination. As travel plans are arranged, and itineraries sent to our mission leaders for review, we always make certain that teams are planning to only drive in the daytime. Why expose teams to such unnecessary risks when good planning makes night travel unnecessary?

Respecting Local Officials & Customs – Getting Permission

This important topic is as much a matter of respect as it is a security issue. All communities, regardless of the socioeconomic conditions, have an individual or group that constitutes their authority structure. Generally it is imperative that approval is obtained from these local authorities for ministries directed to the community. This is especially true for health care teams where involvement of the local health care practitioners and approval of the community health officials is essential for success of the mission.

We are all well aware of short-term mission teams that circumvent approval of local authorities to provide what they believe is an important service that would 'right the wrong' in a developing world community. This shortsightedness may be based more on arrogance than humility, and in addition to being disrespectful, can put the team in very risky situations and potentially jeopardize the ministry. It could lead to a legal entanglement or even arrest.

An important aside for physicians and nurses on medical mission teams: It is a good idea to bring copies of medical school diplomas and licenses. You may be asked for proof that you are a licensed practitioner. Again, never assume that you are able to practice medicine on a trip, even in the developing world.

The bottom line: Although there are some definite exceptions, we recommend obtaining as much governmental permission as possible prior to your departure. This includes approval for activities by local government officials as well as central officials. Assumptions that downplay the role of these local authorities can lead to real difficulties for the team.

Insurance Considerations

Traveler's insurance is of utmost importance for all teams. We recommend that the church purchase coverage for each team so all can have a standardized benefit package as well as the same insurance contact person. All teams having the same insurance agent contacts, as well as the same policy, make it much easier for the CMT in the event of a crisis.

Minimum benefits include: *Medical Accidental, Sickness Coverage, Accidental Death and Dismemberment, Medical Evacuation, Return of Mortal Remains.* Additional coverage can be purchased such as *Trip Interruption* and *Lost Baggage.* When shopping for insurance, consider whether this insurance is secondary to your personal insurance or primary travel insurance and then evaluate which is best for your team or church.

While researching this book, we came across an organization known as the Missionary Travel Association (MTA). The MTA owns the specialized jets that insurance companies contract for medical evacuations. They have an inexpensive subscription program where in the event of a medical emergency requiring evacuation, the MTA is contacted directly which may reduce evacuation time substantially. They repatriate the patient as opposed to evacuating a patient to an appropriate hospital which may be in another foreign country. Churches and agencies should consider organizations such as this that can provide high quality and efficient support. You can research MTA at www.missionarytravelassociation.com.

Regarding van or automobile insurance, it is important to check with your insurance agent to make certain your coverage is active when outside the U.S. This includes teams traveling to Canada and Mexico. Don't assume because you are taking a church bus or van to Mexico that you are adequately insured once you cross the border. Some policies have exceptions, so it is imperative that you verify in your pre-trip planning.

Since driving in some European countries might be exceptions to a "no drive" policy, it is important to make certain you have appropriate insurance that is in effect in each country. Check with your insurance company before you depart. In Canada, your insurance might cover your private auto only if you notify your carrier ahead of time.

Registration With the U.S. State Department

When the earthquake occurred in Haiti on January 12, 2010, the United States had a massive relief and evacuation effort. U.S. Military transports evacuated many people in a short time. Typically, those who are evacuated quickly are those who have registered online with the State Department at https://travelregistration. state.gov. By registering, the State Department knows they are in the country, where they are, and how to get in touch with them. Many of the U.S. embassies are using text messaging to contact people since this often works even when the cell phone systems are not functioning.

As important as these reasons are, there is one additional important risk-related reason why it is important to register with the State Department prior to leaving home: There is a release of information form on the website that needs to be completed permitting the embassy to provide information to family members, friends or churches on a traveler in-country. Only then can a local embassy legally release information on a team or team member in trouble in the country. Can you imagine how awkward it would be if for privacy reasons you are unable to obtain updates on your team in the midst of a crisis? Don't forget – add this imperative to your pre-trip planning. By both registering and authorizing the release of Privacy Act information, you can specific your CMT under "other" on the automated form. The online process is easy to complete and now requires little time.

Chapter 10

Health Considerations

Overview

Taking steps to prevent a health crisis starts before the team departs. As mentioned in the preceding chapter, the health of team members is an important consideration during the recruitment phase of trip planning. Other considerations to assist the team in maintaining good health would include vaccination updates, discussing prophylactic medicines, consider personal needs and finally, providing the team with a well-equipped medical kit.

Most health problems incurred by the team likely will be more of an incident than a crisis. For example, although traveler's diarrhea will put a team member on the sideline for 24-48 hours, such an illness would likely not jeopardize the mission and thus would be considered an *incident* – albeit a frustrating and temporarily debilitating incident for the individual.

However, health care crises do happen, and generally, many are avoidable. A person suffering a heart attack because he or she wasn't used to the increased salt in the diet or the physical strain of carrying heavy luggage can most certainly become a crisis. The person having a severe asthma attack in a high altitude situation can be a life-threatening emergency. A severe injury necessitating hospitalization in a developing world facility could potentially become a crisis.

Water, Water Everywhere – But Not a Drop to Drink!

The majority of traveler's diarrhea is from water contaminated with bacteria, parasites, and very problematic - tiny viruses. It generally is not the exotic food that creates illness; it truly is all about the water.

This has obvious implications to the mission team traveling outside the United States. Drinking water – even bottled water – is probably the number one cause of sickness in a foreign field. So:

DON'T DRINK THE BOTTLED WATER WITHOUT PURIFYING IT!

There is a widespread myth that all bottled water is safe. Team leaders have told me that in the past they used to sterilize the water using various modalities, but unfortunately with the availability of bottled water they have stopped.

To maintain a team's good health during the trip, it is essential that team members drink only purified water. While we can trust major airlines and a few major cities to have purified water (e.g. London and Paris), it is imperative that water from other cities is considered potentially infectious. Importantly, this includes all bottled water in other countries. Even recognized U.S. brands distributed in foreign markets are not to be trusted since frequently they are bottled locally adhering only to the local standards. Regardless of what you are told, the team should purify all bottled water in a foreign field! Water safety is one of few areas that we do not rely on the advice of the field hosts. While they might have the best of intentions in keeping the team hydrated, they may not understand the risks from the bottled water that they supply to the team.

There are several ways to decontaminate water from unregulated sources, but to remove tiny viruses, the process must purify and not just filter the water. Probably the most convenient is the SteriPEN©[xiii] as shown in the picture. This instrument kills all infectious agents in 48 to 90 seconds (depending on the volume), including the tiny viral particles, by an ultraviolet light. It is the size of a sunglass case and can be purchased at travel stores or online starting around $60. To make it easier for users, the most recent models use AA batteries, so we suggest a team always carry extra batteries. The squeeze Katadyn MyBottle©,[xiv] with its three stage Virustat purifier core, is also very effective and reliable. The three stage Virustat filter (not just the two stage Microfilter) is a must to ensure viruses are removed. We carry both on trips to ensure we always are able to purify water. There are other purifying systems available including boiling water, but which ever process is selected the key is to make certain the process kills viruses.

Lee: I was on one trip to a developing country where several U.S.

teams stayed and ate together at a local hotel. All teams, except for our team, drank bottled water or water from the hotel water cooler. We used the SteriPEN© to purify all the water we drank. After five days, all the teams had a minimum of a third of their team members develop gastroenteritis; nobody on our team got sick. Our team had the Bible in one hand (Ephesians 6:17) and the SteriPEN© in the other!

Another case in point: A large metro-Atlanta church recently sent a team to Russia. One of the members knew of our work in preparing short-term mission teams and asked for advice. Of course our first question was: "What water do you plan to drink?" The response was as expected, "bottled water." We provided her with a purifier, along with an admonition to avoid unpurified bottled water and ice, and encouraged her to have the team leader take similar steps to protect the team. She stayed healthy during the trip and was able to minister each day in the field, unlike several of her team who became ill – most likely from the unpurified bottled water they drank.

As these stories confirm, if a team uses one of these purifier systems, avoids ice, and does not consume fruits and vegetables washed in potentially contaminated water, the chances of acquiring disabling gastroenteritis are lessened significantly.

What about Pepto-Bismol tablets? While it does decrease the incidence of traveler's diarrhea, such high doses are required that it is generally not a viable option for most teams.

Finally, well water and mountain streams should be considered contaminated and for that reason are not exceptions to the rule. We have heard that nationals in the field have offered teams well water that they say is "clean well water, clear and free of disease." Some of the worse infections can come from wells and streams, including a parasite called *Giardia.* [xv] I [Lee] remember the pastor who acquired *Giardia* in just this way during a short-term trip in the 1980s. This unfortunate person to this day has residual intestinal problems caused by this 'clean water.'

It is unusual for our team members to become ill while in the field if they follow these recommendations. When we are leading teams, we feel that we have failed any team member who gets gastroenteritis. It is absolutely preventable.

No — it's not the food. No — it's not the climate. Yes— it's caused by the impure, bottled water you drank. While intriguing and exciting, food in other countries rarely causes health problems. So remember — to avoid traveler's diarrhea, *It's all about the water!*

Vaccinations

The CDC website[xvi] provides the most reliable vaccination requirements for the traveler. Here is an overview that might help you understand the vaccination requirements for most teams.

Pertussis-Diphtheria-Tetanus – A booster every ten years is the recommended interval.

Hepatitis A – An excellent vaccine. The first shot protects for two years and a booster (the same vaccine) within 6-24 months of the first provides a lifetime of protection. Commonly individuals forget the booster and have to start the series of two shots over again.

Hepatitis B – A series of three expensive shots that are recommended by the CDC and travel clinics. However, I [Lee] do not recommend this vaccination for mission teams since promiscuity is not an issue on a mission trip and blood transfusions would be a remote possibility. I would only recommend it for dentists or other health professionals who are exposed to blood, and typically they are already vaccinated. With that said, as with hepatitis A vaccination, most youth now are getting immunized as part of their school vaccinations.

Typhoid – Another good vaccination that travelers should consider. The shot protects for three years and the pills for five years. The challenge with the pills is that, not too surprisingly, the person must actually ingest them! Leaving the pills in their car will not protect a person from typhoid. So – if there is any question of compliance – the shot should be the first choice.

Adult Polio Booster – Recommended for certain specific fields. Check the CDC travel page for the details.

Influenza Immunization – We forget that while influenza is a problem in the winter months of North America, other countries in the southern hemisphere have their influenza season during our summer. With this in mind, the team member in July returning from Ecuador with a flu-like illness (fevers, aches and pains, fatigue) may in fact have influenza. I have seen short-term teams become fairly disabled when a flu-like illness spreads through an unvaccinated team. For these reasons, we encourage individuals contemplating a mission trip in the summer to receive the seasonal influenza vaccination when it is available in the preceding fall.

Malaria Prophylaxis

If the CDC (http://www.cdc.gov/travel) says you need to take prophylaxis – then you need it – it should not be negotiable. As you can see from the CDC website, the destination determines the medicine options. The accompanying table highlights the most commonly used prophylactic malaria medication available.

TABLE
Malarial Preventative Medications

Medicine	Advantage	Disadvantage
Lariam	Weekly	Expensive Uncommon but bothersome side effect
Malarone	Well tolerated	Daily
Doxycycline	Inexpensive	Daily; A lot of pills for a long time; not in children less than 8 y/o; increases sun sensitivity – uncommon but a bothersome side effect
Chloroquine	Weekly & Well tolerated	Only in limited destinations

Lee: I can tell you I have cared for many patients over the years who had visited a malaria-infested area and became infected with malaria. This should not happen in the era of good, available prophylactic medication. All too often it is because of minor gastrointestinal upset and the traveler stops taking the pills. Another reason might be that the local host told them it was not necessary to take medicine "since most people here don't do that." This erroneous message has caused a lot of problems and for that reason we coach our team members not to stop their medication for any reason. Parents of children less than ten and pregnant women going on a mission trip need to consult their physicians to discuss their best options for malaria prophylaxis.

While we're on the subject, in addition to taking preventative pills, it is a good idea to follow the non-medicine advice provided by the CDC. This includes long sleeve shirts after dark, repellant, and mosquito nets. These not only help decrease exposure to malaria but also to other infections carried by mosquitoes.

One final crisis-related comment on malaria: Over the years I have had numerous phone calls from travelers in Africa telling me that they were sick and were told that they had acquired malaria. They are quite reassured when I tell them that the timing and their prophylactic medication would make malaria extremely unlikely and that they have some other minor infectious problem. This scenario happens frequently because it is common among Africans to attribute any illness to malaria. This awareness might reassure the team and make it less likely a trip would end because someone got 'malaria.'

Preventative Antibiotics

As an infectious disease physician, I frequently get asked whether or not I would recommend individuals take antibiotic prophylaxis to prevent bacterial diarrhea during a short-term mission trip. I recall an experience several years ago during a medical conference held for infectious disease specialists in Mexico. Following a lecture admonishing these physicians to refrain for various reasons from giving their patients prophylactic antibiotics, the speaker asked the specialists to hold up their hand if they were taking prophylactic antibiotics during the conference. Almost every hand went up! This illustrates just how complex, and somewhat discretionary, the factors are in determining whether or not to take an antibiotic.

There are several issues that have discouraged me from recommending prophylactic antibiotics for all situations. Here are some pertinent caveats that should help short-term teams deliberating whether or not they should all take an antibiotic each day they are serving in a foreign country.

Factors to consider:
- Antibiotics will not prevent all traveler's diarrhea since viruses that are not killed by antibiotics can cause it.
- Antibiotics may give team members a false sense of security, leading team members to think – *we can drink this water since we are taking an antibiotic.*
- Every medicine has a side effect – and these antibiotics are no exception. Ciprofloxacin is commonly used and is generally well tolerated. However, one side effect that is frustrating and can cause real problems is muscle and tendon inflammations that may be manifested by joint and muscle pain. Additionally ciprofloxacin is not recommended for children.

Dr. Lee's recommendations:
- Avoid using prophylactic antibiotics in most situations.
- If you will be in very difficult and primitive living and eating conditions, then each team member can discuss the circumstance and possible prophylactic antibiotics with their personal doctors.
- If it is decided to take a medicine, for team members over 12 years of age, Ciprofloxacin 250mg each day while in the field may be indicated. Dosing prior to arriving in the field is not indicated.

Dehydration

Dehydration is a major risk for short-term travelers. Airplane travel, a dry environment where they are serving, and the unavailability of good water are contributing factors. Add a mild concurrent illness such as a head cold or diarrhea and the problem is magnified. Here is the challenge: There are no clear-cut symptoms that would alert the individual of developing dehydration. Unexplained headaches in a hot, humid setting would suggest that either lack of fluid intake or loss of fluid or both has caused the problem.

Steve's experience is an excellent illustration of this problem.

"On a recent mission trip, I worked at an altitude of 5000 feet continuously for the week; the air was dry and with a fairly even temperature in the mid 70s F. Black tea and green tea were plentiful at this time as well as the occasional instant coffee and some cola and orange soda. Embarrassingly enough, we were on a medical trip and one of the prescribed remedies for the local people was to drink more water. Well, I thought I was getting enough fluid, yet my intake did not equal my output and the water level in my purified bottle did not seem to go down very much. To make the situation even more embarrassing, it was my birthday and the team had taken me to a restaurant for dinner and cake. There was a blazing fireplace nearby and, of course, I was seated near it. I was flushed, hot, dry, cold, clammy and nauseous all at the same time to the extent that I had to get a ride back to our lodging. Dinner was great for the team and my birthday went off without a hitch, but without me. Thankfully, after drinking several liters of water, I was back to normal within two hours. The moral of this story...don't neglect the basics of staying

healthy. There is nothing worse than flying halfway around the world to lie sick in bed from an ailment that was very preventable and self-induced."

Steve's story highlights the important admonition about dehydration – it is a subtle problem that can sneak up on a person insidiously and cause a myriad of non-specific problems. We are all usually aware of the risks of dehydration in hot, humid environments, but forget just how dehydrating high altitude can be. The avoidance of dehydration makes another argument for the water purifiers we discussed above. Having adequate volumes of purified water available is of paramount importance to maintain good health while traveling, and having purifiers available expands the sources of water available to the team.

One additional suggestion to encourage good hydration: At the U.S. airport, after security clearance and prior to boarding for your last leg before the destination, buy a liter bottle of water for each team member. Not only does this insure that each person would have a reusable water bottle available while traveling, but it provides an option for those who are not 'water drinkers,' that is people who get bored drinking just plain water. Encourage them to bring individual serving dry powders in various flavors. They can use the spare bottle to mix the powder so they will have flavored water to keep hydrated.

Special Note for Construction Teams

Construction teams laboring in the hot and humid climates are especially at risk for severe dehydration. The intense water, salt and electrolyte loss can be striking and lead to a major health crisis. The situation can be magnified when you consider volunteers on construction trips who are not physically used to such work. Lee: During my time recently with a medical team in a hot and humid field, I witnessed first-hand a couple of members of a construction team from a different church become severely dehydrated, including one whose dehydrated state might have rapidly become life threatening. While working on construction teams, drinking liters of sports drinks and purified water, possibly along with daily salt tablets, should prevent severe dehydration from developing.

As an aside, construction standards in some countries can be very lax. So while you are watching your fluid intake, also make sure you are working safely, not necessarily like the gentlemen in this photo.

And Each Team Member - Don't Forget to Bring with You...

- All your necessary personal medications – labeled bottles in your carry-on and a set in your check-in luggage.
- A copy of your recent cardiogram if you have had any cardiac ailments.
- Your daily aspirin if suggested by your doctor.
- Your SteriPEN© and Katadyne© water purifiers.

Section IV

In the Field

Change 11

Situational Awareness

There are many things a team can do to mitigate risk during a mission trip. As we have already said, it all starts with prayer support including pre-trip prayer preparation and enlisting prayer warriors at home to be daily lifting up the team while the team is in the field. Add to prayer support situational awareness, that is being constantly vigilant of the potential risks in the environment, and throw in a healthy dose of common sense, and the building blocks are in place for a safe experience.

Vigilance in the Field

As anyone trained in security would tell you, it is imperative that there is constant vigilance. This awareness not only involves scrutiny of people, but it also involves the physical environment. If a crisis is to be averted, all team members must be on the lookout for risky situations – not just the team leader. It is amazing what we can learn just by observing our surroundings. Are you being followed? Is the fire escape locked?

Sometimes when team leaders travel to countries on a regular basis, they may become complacent and let their guard down because of the comfort of familiar settings. This false sense of security can potentially place teams at significant risk.

An Unusual Commotion? Watch Your Belongings!

In the same way a magician distracts an audience in order to carry out a trick, pick pocket thieves rely on some commotion to work their trade. Lee: A few years back in Barcelona, I was on an escalator exiting a subway. At the top, an individual dropped a pile of subway tickets that caused the crowd to bump into each other as they attempted to step off the escalator. During the commotion, my wallet was removed. Obviously, one person caused the distraction by dropping useless tickets while the other did the stealing. Fortunately I caught the person, got my wallet back and learned a good lesson: if an unusual commotion happens in a public area, hold onto your belongings, a thief may be at work. Better yet, secure your belongings so this cannot happen.

Going For a Walk – *Be Aware!*

Can you imagine you are walking on a dark street in India with your fellow short-termer who suddenly disappears from sight? When you hear the cry for help, you realize your friend has fallen through an open manhole cover! Someone stole the manhole cover for the metal content. Without a doubt, a large hole in the sidewalk can cause substantial injury.

Walking in Africa, or maybe in a hundred other places, it might not be uncommon to be near an open drainage ditch alongside what would be a sidewalk. Open ditches, grated covers, raised blocks on a sidewalk, and holes in the side-walk all present hazards that we might not be used to seeing. In this African scene the drainage ditch is half the height of this person who is over six feet tall. This is why we discourage team members from going out in the dark.

Fire hydrants are usually there for our protection, but walking into this hydrant in the middle of the sidewalk, day or night, could cause a significant injury.

Cute Animals – Terrible Bites!

You probably would not allow your child to pet an unknown dog through a fence, so why would you want to do it in a foreign land? Rabies is endemic in many locations around the world, so dogs, domestic or wild, should be avoided.

How about accepting the opportunity to hold a large eagle or falcon on the side of a road in the mountains of Central Asia? Probably not a wise thing to be doing. You can be certain there are no quality control or safety

standards that you have come to expect from a vendor in the United States.
Notice the eagle's long, strong talons and large beak. One startled bird could to lead to severe eye trauma or other injuries. Looks like fun, but we suggest you avoid such risky adventures.

How about the offer to hold those cute little monkeys in a world market place? Monkey bites can lead to severe infections so it is prudent to stay away from them. Steve: My father once told me of a story during World War II where one of his fellow airmen had a "tame" monkey on a leash. One day that monkey jumped on the airman's shoulder and promptly bit him on the back of the neck. Frequently, market place monkeys bite tourists and then a hectic search for the monkey's rabies vaccination record ensues. This search inevitably ends with the realization that there is no way these animals are vaccinated. The only option now is for the person with the bite wound to receive a series of painful rabies vaccinations. The same risk scenario would play out for a dog bite.

Bottom line: Consider all birds and animals encountered during your short-term mission trip as potentially dangerous.

Other Settings for Injuries

We send a number of youth trips each year to one location in Central America. This is one of most traveled locations because of the very high quality experience and the overall relative safety of the trip. However, during a recent trip one of the young team members went out by himself to jump on a trampoline. It was twenty minutes before he was missed and then was found on the trampoline with significant injuries to his knee. Trampolines are dangerous at home and in the field.

Climbing trees, getting on roofs, riding motor scooters, use your imagination about what would be wise not to do. Remembering that quality health care may not be readily available in a foreign field, potential high-risk activities should be avoided even if it is something that might be undertaken back home. Common sense is your best ally.

Lodging – *Is it Safe?*

It is not uncommon to read about tragedies in the U.S. when people die after being trapped in houses that are enveloped in fire and smoke. If this can happen in America in the setting of extensive fire regulations, it most certainly can happen in countries with less rigid rules. For that reason, you need to be aware of the fire hazards in hotels in the developing world. In these settings, there are generally no fire doors, but rather locked doors to keep people from getting in while inadvertently preventing people from exiting. At a hotel, every team member should make sure that they can easily exit a building that might be a potential fire-trap.

These environmental hazards could turn a short-term trip into a crisis situation when a severe fracture or infected animal bite necessitates medical evacuation to a country with modern hospitals.

Crisis prevention in the field is all about common sense and vigilance of all team members.

Chapter 12

A Crisis in the Field

―∞∞―

A Crisis Occurs - Initial Field Response

When a crisis does occur, the team leader's training should take over. He or she would make certain the team is in a safe environment while reminding them that God has promised to be with them – and He is! Secondly, the CMT is then immediately contacted by satellite or cell phone and informed about the nature of the crisis. The CMT will then work with the team leader to take any necessary steps to resolve the situation, and will notify the families as well as appropriate church leaders. During this time, the team leader will be the only person communicating from the field.

The Ministry Ends and the Team Goes Home

Once the immediate crisis has been resolved, the ministry is now over and the CMT will assist the team leader in initiating the necessary logistics to bring the team home. There is no benefit to leaving the team in the field to debrief or to have any group counseling sessions. Since team leaders and team members generally are not equipped to provide appropriate counseling, the primary focus should be to provide comfort and encouragement to the team and to get them home to receive appropriate professional counseling.

Stateside Pre-Return Planning

As we learned from our ineptness in dealing with our 2005 experience, appropriately supporting the team when they return home after experiencing a crisis should be planned in detail. Since their initial responses may greatly impact the team members' recovery, the CMT, church leaders and family members have a responsibility in preparing for the team to return. With that in mind, it is very important that representatives of the church's crisis management team consult with family members to discuss each team member prior to their return home so they could anticipate how the team member might be dealing with situation. For example, you might ask *"do you think your son will verbalize his feelings or will he probably keep his feelings to himself?"*

Depending on the situation, the church should retain a qualified professional counselor to provide advice to the family and church leaders prior to the team's return.

Caring for the Member Returning Home after a Crisis

There are several important considerations to prepare for the homecoming of a team that has undergone a crisis during their trip. Although all situations are different, and not all team members are impacted in the same way, there are some fairly universal approaches.

First of all, it is important not to minimize how you believe the team might be affected by the crisis. Each individual will probably be processing the adverse experience in his or her own unique way, and some may be more traumatized than others. We have learned that the best approach is to proceed as if each member has been profoundly impacted by the experience. Better to be overly concerned and be proven wrong, than the alternative of downplaying the impact.

We have also learned how important it is to have church leaders meet the team when they arrive at the airport. We have under-valued this in the past. Demonstrating real caring starts when the team first steps foot back on American soil. Depending on the severity of the crisis, consider meeting the team outside the U.S. and escorting them home.

Post-Crisis Counseling

Professional counseling for the team as a group might be the important first step. Additionally, counseling for each individual would in all likelihood be recommended.

Will your church cover the costs of the counseling? We have made the determination to cover any necessary group counseling sessions but in the future not to cover individual counseling sessions. Our reasoning is since we do not provide financial coverage for a team member returning with a fractured leg, we likewise would not cover emotional care. We would provide assistance if an individual has financial needs, but this would be the exception not the rule. Whatever approach your CMT program takes, it is important that there is a policy reflecting this question of counseling coverage.

One last emphasis on post-crisis counseling: Amateurs should not play counselors but rather seek the guidance of professionals qualified in this area.

Section V

Resting Our Case

Chapter 13

Let the Dialogue Begin!

―⊶―

The Plan in Action

Around the time we were sending this manuscript to the publishers early in 2010, we were called to respond to one of the most devastating disasters ever to strike the western hemisphere – the earthquake in Haiti.

As we prepared to send out disaster relief teams, we instituted the basic tenants of our crisis program. We first weighed potential risks a relief team in Haiti would be exposed to. The complexities and challenges of security were quite obvious during the many hours of television coverage, so it was an issue that we considered in some detail. We then considered the actual ministry of the team – specifically what do they intend to accomplish during their time in Haiti. We felt that providing medical care and supplies to Haitians, while providing encouragement to the worn out church leaders constituted a very compelling reason to go. As we balanced the potential risks with the ministry objectives, it was quite clear – this disaster relief team needed to go to Haiti.

We then turned to team member recruitment. We felt that a team of six to eight members would be best when security, travel and housing issues were considered. Since the team was to provide medical relief, we decided that a few non-medical members and four to five medical personnel would be ideal.

Also, following our guidelines, we registered with the State Department, had extensive discussions with the hosts in the field, and held our team member preparation meetings to prepare the team. The ministry objective – to encourage the local Haitian pastors – was always in the forefront of our deliberations, while discussions on security precautions were included at all team meetings.

All of this was possible because of the experiences we have had for the past few years in preparing teams for the mission fields. Sending disaster relief teams without the preparation that we have outlined in this book would not only put team members at potential risk, but could put well intended and poorly prepared people into a disaster field with the possibility that they might compromise the rescue efforts of professional responders.

Closing

We do hope that churches and short-term mission sending agencies will be convicted that they need to institute some type of similar crisis prevention program so that more can go as commanded by the Lord – and go effectively and safely.

Our prayer is that the North American churches sending millions of short-term missionaries throughout the world will heed our admonition, and take these specific steps – not for their sake, but for the sake of the One who calls people to ministry.

As we mentioned in the preface to this book, our intent is to encourage churches to identify this issue as a priority so that a movement on crisis prevention will ensue and a nationwide dialogue will happen as we continue to go as commanded *to all nations.*

Let the dialogue begin!

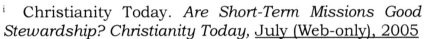

i Christianity Today. *Are Short-Term Missions Good Stewardship? Christianity Today,* July (Web-only), 2005
ii Lausanne World Pulse – *What's Happening in Short-term Mission?* Roger Peterson March 2006.
iii Christianity Today (Web-only). 2007 Strong Support for Danger Zone Missions
iv Churches that went: Christian Medical Dental Association. Personal communication.
v Churches that stayed home: Gaithersburg Church of the Nazarene, Gaithersburg, MD. Website.
vi Churches that came home early: The CDP International Mission Team. Trip Report
vii *Voices of the Faithful.* Beth Moore. 2005. International Board of the Southern Baptist Convention. Integrity Publishers.
viii *Disaster Responses? Is the US Really Prepared.* L. Jacobs, The Permanente Journal Vol. 10. No 3. Fall 2006
ix *You Can Tell the World,* The Living God is a Missionary God," John Stott Intervarsity Christian Fellowship/USA. Intervarsity Press. 1979
x Experiencing God Day-by-Day. Henry T. Blackaby and Richard Blackaby. Broadman & Holman Publishers. February 9th Devotional. 1997.

[xi] Vereb, Hitt & Associates, Woodstock, GA. Information: www.verebhitt.com; email steve@verebhitt.com for more information or to order risk assessments.
[xii] http://wwwnc.cdc.gov/travel/yellowbook/2010/chapter-2/injuries-safety.aspx
[xiii] SteriPEN©. www.steripen.com
[xiv] Katadyne©. www.katadyne.com
[xv] Giardia: http://www.cdc.gov/healthywater/drinking/private/wells/disease/giardia.html
[xvi] CDC web site: http://www.cdc.gov/travel)

TEAM MEDICAL KITS
*** Call Dr. Lee Jacobs for specific directions ***

Trip: _____Leader: _____
Signed out:_____Signed in: _____

Please note if you used any of the contents so they can be replaced:

Pain:
- **Ibuprofen - 200mg** - Take 2 every 4 hours as needed. Take with food.
- **Tylenol Extra Strength** - Take 2 every 4 hours as needed.
- **Tylenol #3 w/codeine** - Take 1-2 every four hours for severe pain.

Diarrhea:
- **Ciprofloxin - 500mg** - Twice a day for severe, persistent diarrhea as directed by MDs.
- **Imodium** - For severe, persistent diarrhea - take 1 every hour up to 5 a day.
- **Lomotil** - For severe diarrhea that persists despite the Imodium.

Nausea:
- **Phenergan - 25mg** - Take 1 every 6 hours for nausea and vomiting.

Antibiotic for Infection:
- **Bactrim DS (Sulfur)** - Twice a day as directed by MDs.
- **Doxycycline - 100mg** - Twice a day as directed by MDs.

- **Keflex - 500mg** - Take 1 pill 3x a day for infection as directed by MDs.

Other Infections:

- **Antifungal cream** - For fungal skins rashes.
- **Garamycin Ophthalmic Cream** - Twice a day on lower lid for crusted conjunctivitis.
- **Monistat** - For yeast vaginitis.

Allergy:

- **Albuterol Inhaler** - For asthmatic-type wheezing as directed by MDs.
- **Benadryl 25mg** - Take 1 every 4 hours for itching or congestion.
- **Epipen** - For injection in emergency acute reactions (eg. bee sting) - especially if swollen with breathing difficulty.
- **Hydrocortisone 2.5% cream** - For itching rash. Apply 4 times a day.
- **Prednisone 10mg** - For severe allergic reaction: only with MD direction.

Cold:

- **Pseudoephedrine** - Primarily for cold but also allergy/sinus. Take 2 every 6 hours.
- **Afrin nasal spray** - If flying with a cold, use before take offs and landings.

Miscellaneous:

- **Ace wrap**
- **Bandaids**
- **Betadine swabs**
- **Temporary dental filling packs**

9 781609 575205